USING STUDENT TEAMS IN THE CLASSROOM

A Faculty Guide

RUTH FEDERMAN STEIN
SANDRA HURD

Syracuse University

Foreword by Mara Sapon-Shevin

ANKER PUBLISHING COMPANY, INC.
Bolton, Massachusetts

Using Student Teams in the Classroom
A Faculty Guide

ISBN 1-882982-37-1

Composition by Lyn Rodger, Deerfoot Studios
Cover design by Delaney Design

Anker Publishing Company, Inc.
176 Ballville Road
P. O. Box 249
Bolton, MA 01740-0249

www.ankerpub.com

About the Authors

RUTH FEDERMAN STEIN interviewed Sandra Hurd for her dissertation, *Conditions that Facilitate the Implementation of Innovative Freshman Experience Courses.* At that time Sandy, as part of her course load, taught and advised a recitation section in Syracuse University's School of Management introductory management course. Later she became the course director and worked with Ruth on the course manual and a handbook on teamwork in college that evolved into this book.

Ruth currently works at the Center for Support of Teaching and Learning at Syracuse University. Some of her activities include organizing Focus on Teaching sessions for faculty, helping to coordinate the university's Vision Fund project, and working with faculty to improve teaching and learning on the campus.

SANDRA HURD is department chair and professor of law and public policy in the School of Management at Syracuse University and serves as faculty coordinator of the university's learning communities program. She continues to direct the freshman management course and developed a learning community program for first-year students in management.

Contents

Part I: Teamwork Theory and Discussion

Part II: Building Effective Teams

Part III: Teamwork in the Disciplines

Part IV: Articles/Resources

Foreword

Students are seated in a large lecture hall. But rather than looking forward and listening to a professor lecturing, they are arranged in groups of four, their heads bent over a problem. "If we organize it according to the population of the school," says one student, "then we could calculate the relative literacy rates according to size and location." "But," interjects another student, "we really have to talk about the socioeconomic levels of the school neighborhoods to understand the different kinds of literacy being discussed here." A third student volunteers, "I'm Puerto Rican, and Spanish is my native language. Wouldn't it be important to discuss what literacy means in places where English might be a second language for some students?" The fourth student adds, "I think we have lots of ideas here—let's begin to make a list of all the factors that would affect our calculations."

There are 30 such groups spread around the lecture hall, and the hum of talk is constant. But it's clearly a productive noise—students talking, listening, engaged. At the end of 20 minutes, when the professor calls the groups back together, drawing their attention to the front of the room, every student has spoken and been listened to, and many ideas have been raised, critiqued, and analyzed. The complexity of the task has been significantly increased; none of the groups thinks the task is as simple as when they began. The subsequent lecture—about poverty, literacy, social justice, and race—will be far richer than it would have been before the group interaction. Students will no doubt raise many of the concerns the professor herself would have identified for the group, but the issues will be owned and personalized by the students and groups who raised them. Could this be a college classroom? It certainly doesn't sound like the experience many of us had in institutions of higher education.

These are exciting times in higher education. Not only has there been increased attention to what gets taught to students in colleges and universities, but there is also growing awareness of how teaching is enacted and learning achieved. Furthermore, changes in these two areas are linked, calling on us for congruence and compatibility between what and how we teach.

The recognition that we live in a diverse, multicultural society has made it critical that students be exposed to a wide range of differences throughout their college years. We are no longer satisfied with courses and programs that privilege only dominant cultural, religious, and ethnic groups or that assume that all people are of the same socioeconomic class, have the same sexual preferences, or possess identical abilities and disabilities.

We want all students to be comfortable and knowledgeable about the multiple forms of difference that strengthen and enrich our society, able to adapt their thinking and extend their reach beyond the obvious or the commonplace. Because of this goal, many colleges and universities now require courses in multicultural literature or include a diversity requirement within their degree programs. The goal of preparing all students to be members of a community—or multiple communities—reclaiming their civic responsibilities is increasingly identified as critical for tomorrow's citizens.

This focus on living and working in a diverse society also has major implications for how we teach students. The days in which a faculty member stood in front of a large group of students in a lecture hall, reading from a text or delivering a nonstop presentation are fast disappearing. Not only do we have considerable evidence that this teaching style is often ineffective, but we also have a growing body of research that supports the importance of students learning and working together. When students work together in small learning groups, or teams, the benefits are both cognitive and social.

As *Using Student Teams in the Classroom* demonstrates, there is ample evidence for the need to teach students to work together, giving and receiving information, offering support and encouragement, negotiating conflict, and learning to communicate effectively. It is undeniable that the product of a truly cooperative successful partnership or group is often far superior to what any one individual—no matter how smart—could have done by himself or herself.

The poster that reads "None of us is as smart as all of us" is well documented in this volume.

But simply placing students in groups and imploring them to cooperate is not enough. Students require specific skills to negotiate their way through group process. What happens when one student dominates the group and won't allow other voices? What do we do about students who sit back and are passive or resistant? How can tasks be designed that genuinely demand the full participation and engagement of every student in the group? And how do we evaluate group work in ways that are both meaningful and fair? These are some of the many questions explored in *Using Student Teams in the Classroom*. This volume will be of tremendous value to other faculty who are trying to revise and rework their curricula and teaching so that students are more actively engaged with the material and with one another.

If we want students to be prepared to work in a multicultural, diverse workplace, to live in neighborhoods that cross ethnic and racial boundaries, then we must make sure that not only what we teach but how we teach affirms the importance of learning to work together.

No matter what we teach, it is important that students be fluent with the content, able to discuss, analyze, and critique their ideas and support their thinking. Students must be able to hear different voices, consider others' opinions, and integrate multiple perspectives. While standing one's ground is an important character strength, the ability to negotiate, compromise, and seek yet another solution is equally important.

There is virtually no job that is performed in isolation. Twenty years ago, when faced with a student with cognitive competence but poor social skills, the standard response was "Well, he/she can become a computer expert and just deal with machines and not people." But the reality today is that even computer experts find themselves interfacing—not just with machines—but with people. Explaining new operating systems, training employees, and developing new, responsive software all involve working with and communicating well with others. It is hard to think of a single job today that doesn't involve working with others at some level. We can ill afford to graduate students who are competent but uncommunicative, skilled but unable to share those skills, capable of doing but not of teaching what they know.

The examples in *Using Student Teams in the Classroom* are drawn from a wide variety of fields, including architecture, biology, ceramics, engineering, and English. The range of imaginative teaching strategies—all of which include students working in groups—is evidence of the wealth of ways in which cooperative learning can be incorporated in college classrooms. The reader is encouraged to ask, How could I incorporate these teaching strategies in my own teaching? And, perhaps equally important, how can I use the authors of this book and others in my own institution to support my ventures into new forms of pedagogy and curriculum? The authors of the volume have done an excellent job of bringing together diverse examples and interesting applications. These are coupled with a solid explanation of some of the caveats of cooperative learning and deep respect for the ways in which such pedagogical changes will challenge long-held beliefs and practices. The possibilities are endless, the potential benefits are exciting, and the prospect of teaching our students well gives us both impetus and courage. Let us begin.

Mara Sapon-Shevin
Professor of Education, Syracuse University
Past Co-President, The International Association
*   for the Study of Cooperation in Education*

Preface

Feedback from student evaluations as well as faculty experience suggests that both faculty and students need to be better prepared for teamwork in the classroom. Faculty and students have learned that teamwork is not a simple process, but that it requires training, planning, and experience for it to be effective and satisfying.

Organization of the Book

The discussion in Part I of this guide provides an introduction to the theory underlying teamwork and suggests basic ways to think about incorporating teamwork into the college classroom.

Part II contains practical information for anyone who is planning to use teams. There are guidelines that can be used with student teams or adapted for a particular situation. Several examples of exercises are provided for acquainting team members with each other, as well a team charter assignment for starting a long-term team. Also included is material to help students communicate effectively with each other to resolve the inevitable conflicts and misunderstandings that arise when a group of people are working together, and practical information on ways to evaluate teamwork, including the team process that the groups are using. This section ends with a compilation of teaching tips that were written by faculty at the University of Minnesota, Duluth who share their experiences with team learning.

Part III includes discipline-specific examples of teamwork from faculty at Syracuse University. The examples range from architecture to engineering to writing and demonstrate the extensive variety of approaches that faculty have created to incorporate groups in their classes. If you have ideas or examples that have worked well for you, please consider sending them to us for inclusion in a subsequent version of this book.

The final section, Part IV, consists of articles by Rod Chesser (Enhancing Performance in Small Groups) and John Boehrer (Spectators and Gladiators: Reconnecting Students with the Problem), a case study by Barbara Millis that describes a cooperative learning dilemma, and an annotated list of additional resources.

Ruth Federman Stein

Sandra Hurd

Acknowledgments

This book first began as a handbook for Syracuse University faculty in the School of Management who were using project teams in their large introductory freshman course. *Teamwork in College: A Handbook* was developed through a faculty instructional grant prepared by Theodore O. Wallin and Paula Bobrowski. Cheryl Stafford, a student in the School of Management, did the initial research. Charles Howell, a writing program consultant with the School of Management, developed the Teamwork Theory and Discussion in Part I and later wrote the Technology and Teamwork section for the book. Nancy Greer and Stephanie Waterman provided numerous suggestions and helped with proofing the original handbook, and Julie Hall did the original cover design and formatting.

Robert M. Diamond, former assistant vice chancellor and director of Syracuse University's Center for Instructional Development, encouraged us to send a copy of the original handbook to Anker Publishing. We are indebted to Susan Anker for suggesting that we expand the original handbook to include more discipline-specific examples. We are also indebted to the many faculty members at Syracuse University who gave us excellent examples of how they incorporate student teams in their particular disciplines. Special thanks go to Judy Grunert and Ned Deuel for their suggestions, to Bron Adam whose editing recommendations were invaluable, and to Rob Pusch for formatting the final version.

I

Teamwork Theory and Discussion

Teamwork Theory and Discussion

Introduction

Cooperative learning is an educational approach that promotes interaction among students and shared responsibility for academic achievement. This book deals with cooperative learning in college courses. It is applicable at all levels of undergraduate instruction, but it is particularly geared to large lower-division classes.

The specific focus of this book is teamwork. Cooperative learning can take many other forms, but teams are especially well suited to large lower-division classes. Teams socialize students, provide a setting for active participation, and create opportunities to offer and receive help. They establish group loyalties that counteract the sense of anonymity students often feel in large classes. Teams mediate between students' individual experience and the intellectual tasks of the course, providing opportunities for shared reflection. Given these effects, it is not surprising that participation in teams has been found to increase student satisfaction and promote retention.

This segment offers a brief introduction to teams. It provides basic explanations of underlying theory and concepts, surveys the types of teams that can be used in classrooms, reviews the stages of team building, suggests techniques of management and intervention, and presents some ideas for evaluation.

Underlying Theory

Why Is Team Learning Increasing?

Traditionally, college professors have used the lecture method, in which students learn that the authority figure in the classroom is the professor and that they must retain the knowledge that is given to them. However, more and more faculty have been incorporating cooperative learning into their classes in recent years by requiring students to meet in teams and contribute to a team project or a final product. There are several reasons for this increase in team assignments. First, there has been a marked trend for business decisions to be made by work teams rather than by individuals making decisions independently. Business, in general, is using more participative management styles, as are many other institutions.

One of the most important reasons for using team learning is that the growing complexity of our various work environments makes it much more difficult for one person to deal with or research issues and make decisions alone. Team learning, therefore, attempts to introduce students to real world experiences in the classroom. It also changes the traditional boundaries of authority in the classroom by forcing team members to work with each other to make decisions instead of looking to the instructor for answers.

What Is the Historical Basis for Cooperative Learning?

John Dewey emphasized the importance of education for teaching students to live in a democratic society where they work together to solve problems. He stressed the importance of group process and felt the classroom should reflect the process of living in a democracy. Thus, in addition to working cooperatively, Dewey believed students should learn to respect others and to work rationally with each other.

Kurt Lewin, a social psychologist during the 1930s and 1940s, also stressed the importance of group dynamics as a way to understand the behavior of those involved in democratic groups. Morton Deutsch, a student of Lewin's, then developed a theory of cooperation and competition based on Lewin's ideas.

More recently, other researchers have studied cooperative learning, for example, David and Roger Johnson at the University of Minnesota, Shlomo and Yael Sharan at the University of Tel Aviv, and Robert Slavin at Johns Hopkins University. Much of their work focused on grades K–12, but more research is now occurring in higher education. Astin (1993) did a study that involved over 27,000 students at 309 colleges and universities. He concluded that student-student interactions and student-faculty interactions, both essential components in teamwork, were the most important influences on academic success and satisfaction. Cooper et al. (1990) found that cooperative learning is more effective than traditional approaches in improving critical thinking, self-esteem, multicultural relations, and positive social behaviors. In more specific studies, Frierson (1986) reported that nursing students at a predominantly black college who studied cooperatively for their state licensing exams passed their exams at a significantly higher rate than comparable students studying individually. Treisman (1983) found that African American students at the University of California, Berkeley, who worked cooperatively in enrichment sessions outside of class, received calculus course grades more than one letter grade higher than comparable African American students who did not use the enrichment programs. College attrition rates for African American students in the year-long program matched the Berkeley average for all students and were significantly lower for program participants than for comparable African American students not involved in the program.

Davis (1993) states that "students learn best when they are actively involved in the process" (p. 147). She goes on to say that "researchers report that, regardless of the subject matter, students working in small teams tend to learn more of what is taught and retain it longer than when the same content is presented in other instructional formats. Students who work in collaborative groups also appear more satisfied with their classes."

Learning Communities

A team construct that goes beyond the establishment of teams within a classroom is the learning community. Learning communities are intentionally restructured curricula designed to foster a community of learners among students and faculty.

The establishment of learning communities, according to Patrick Hill (1985), is a means for responding to a number of problems affecting higher education. One major concern is the lack of intellectual communication between faculty and students and among students. Closely tied to this issue is the lack of a relationship or connection among courses that students take outside their majors. Another important problem is the discordance between faculty who focus on research and theory in their discipline and students who have been encouraged to be career oriented, who lack a strong interest in academics, and who sit passively through class lectures. Finally, a key issue that learning communities address is the retention rate of students.

Cuseo (1991) mentions several studies that show that more than half of the students who leave college do so during their first year. Research cited by Gabelnick, MacGregor, Matthews, & Smith (1992) indicates that "students enrolling in learning community programs generally exhibit higher retention: It is not atypical for a learning community group to exhibit a 90% to 100% rate of completion in the program." They also state that these students persist in college afterwards "to a higher extent than students not enrolling in learning communities."

Barbara Leigh Smith (1991) describes four basic models for learning communities. The simplest learning community is represented by linked courses, for example, linking a skill course with a content course or linking a literature course with a history course with the same students enrolled in both courses. Another model that is similar to the linked courses is clustered courses, courses with a common theme that are linked to enable a group of students to take the cluster together. Faculty may or may not work together to blend their course content. Freshman Interest Groups (FIGS) are another popular learning community. The FIGS model links three courses around a topic related to the students' intended major or a theme; it also has a peer-advising component. The linkage of these two components creates a community of students. The peer advisor meets with the students on a weekly basis for a discussion session that may include orientation activities and that often is the beginning of study groups. According to Smith, the coordinated studies model is the most radical community learning model because it changes the traditional notion of four separate courses to a fully integrated program that may last a full quarter or even an entire year. In this model, the faculty redesign the entire curriculum with their colleagues. Smith mentions two such programs at Evergreen State College in Washington: "Matter and Motion," a full-year integrated program in physics, chemistry, mathematics, and laboratory computing, and "The Paradox of Progress," a program that probes Western civilization, emphasizing great books in the sciences, social sciences, and the humanities.

Other colleges and universities have incorporated a residential component into their learning communities. This element ensures that the students live in proximity to each other and have the opportunity to continue discussions, study groups, and friendships from their linked classes. For example, as part of the Management Learning Community at Syracuse University, students live on the same floor of one residence hall and take three or four linked classes together.

According to Tinto and Riemer (1998), most learning communities have two basic similarities: shared knowledge and shared knowing. By organizing linked or clustered courses around a theme or primary subject, learning communities build a connected learning experience for students, especially first-year students. They are not taking five discrete courses such as writing, calculus, American history, French, and biology; rather, as a community of learners, they study a connected body of knowledge. The faculty teaching these courses help students make the knowledge connections. Additionally, the students, because they are enrolled in a number of classes together, get to know each other better. The faculty teaching these courses frequently use collaborative and cooperative learning methods, thus requiring students to work together in teams or groups as part of the process.

The Criteria for Successful Teamwork

As every instructor who has tried team projects knows, the quality of team performance varies widely. Simply assigning a group report or other exercise does not guarantee that the members of the teams will exchange ideas and share responsibility. Various criteria can be used to distinguish team exercises that involve genuine cooperation from those that are less productive in this respect. In their 1993 study of college-level instructional strategies, Meyers and Jones suggest that for cooperative learning to take place, an activity must exhibit the following five features:

- a sense of interdependence among team members
- accountability of individual students to both team and instructor
- frequent face-to-face interaction to promote team goals
- development of social skills needed for collaboration
- critical analysis of group processes

Since this list offers an unusually succinct and thorough account of the requirements of cooperative group processes, it will be useful to examine these features in greater detail and to review some of the instructional strategies that promote them. As this discussion will make clear, effective team organization involves not only the appropriate dispositions and effort on the part of students who participate in the exercises, but also a certain technological competence on the part of the instructor. Instructors whose chief pedagogical concern has been the organization and exposition of content rather than the modeling and explanation of intellectual skills will find that they have to expand their repertoire of teaching and planning strategies quite significantly in order to implement team exercises effectively.

Interdependence

Meyers and Jones point out that students must believe that one team member can succeed only if the others succeed. This belief is not created just on the basis of the instructor's exhortation; it must be driven home by experience. The role of the instructor here is not just to assert that the success of the individual depends on the success of the group; she must design, structure, and sequence activities in such a way as to bring about this result. Here are some techniques recommended by Johnson et al. in a widely cited 1991 study of group learning activities.

- Procedural guidelines can be structured to require consensus. Team members must explicitly agree both on their final work product and on the procedures by which it is produced.

- Team members can be assigned roles, such as reader, checker, and encourager. This division of labor requires students to synchronize their activities and thus formally expresses the requirement of cooperation.

- At the level of logistics, team members may be required to share resources and are thus encouraged to work more closely together. (For example, if only one copy of an exercise is distributed, then students have to make arrangements to circulate it, figure out their own ideas, and arrange to share them in a discussion.)

- Individual students are rewarded not only for their own performance but also for the success of the team as a whole.

Accountability

As Meyers and Jones observe, the interdependence of the group on the efforts of each of its members can be reinforced by systems of individual accountability. Students must know in advance that performance will be evaluated individually as well as collectively. They must see the results of the assessment and know what consequences result from varying levels of performance.

- Instructors should design a variety of tests, reviews, and other forms of evaluation, some of which occur early enough in the course to influence subsequent performance and affect group process.

- Assessment vehicles can include individual tests for all students, group papers or presentations, observations of a team meeting by the instructor, or a review of the work of one student selected at random to represent the progress of the team as a whole.

- Students should be encouraged to reflect on the results of the assessment and use them to improve group process. Set aside time for this reflection, figure out fair ways to share information, and suggest how it might be interpreted and used as guidelines for action.

Interaction

Cooperative learning requires frequent face-to-face interaction among students. Their dealings with one another should be friendly, encouraging, and focused on the task at hand. Dividing tasks and working alone on them does not achieve the benefit of cooperative learning. Johnson et al. (1991) observe that lessons and activities can be organized in such a way as to encourage the responsiveness that genuine cooperative learning requires.

- Provide sufficient time for this interaction, appropriate seating arrangements, and a suitable level of supervision and encouragement.

- Team activities can be structured to require specific forms of discussion.

Examples:

Students explain difficult concepts and techniques to one another. The team collaborates on a brief written explanation of the most difficult concepts. The written explanation is read aloud and discussed with the rest of the class.

Students discuss the nature and purpose of a new topic of study. Brief outlines of their conclusions are submitted to the instructor, who refers to them during lectures and class discussion.

Students explore connections between current material and what they have learned in other settings. The instructor circulates, makes notes on the most important connections, and discusses them briefly at the start of the next lecture.

Social Skills

Students often come to college with limited experience in cooperative teamwork, and they often lack relevant social skills. Johnson et al. (1991) recommend that these skills be taught as explicitly and systematically as traditional course content.

- Early in the course, instructors should identify social skills that students are expected to learn (active listening and articulation of differences, for example).

- Some or all of the skills may be represented in terms of roles which may be assigned to team members (for example, leader, moderator, trouble-shooter, or recorder).

- Roles should be rotated, so that students can practice different skills and learn from their classmates' performance.

- Monitor and assess fulfillment of the roles, as well as other evidence of the development of social skills.

Group Processing

A number of scholars who study cooperative learning emphasize the importance of processing or reflective discussion (Meyers & Jones, 1993; Johnson et al., 1991; Sharan & Sharan, 1992; Graves & Graves, 1989). Teams should regularly review their performance, reflect on the interaction of their members, and make plans to improve coordination.

- Provide the time and guidance needed for effective processing.

- Explain both the immediate and long-range purpose for processing, and emphasize its importance to the development of social skills.

- Structure the process by specifying questions to be addressed and procedures to be employed. Activities should be varied to avoid letting students slip into a routine.

- Results of processing should be shared among teams and discussed by the class as a whole.

Some Basic Configurations of Teams

Instructors tend to think of teams in terms of a standard format and project type. In doing so, however, they may significantly underestimate the pedagogical contribution that team exercises can make to a course. Teams come in a variety of configurations, and team activities vary widely, depending on instructional needs, the amount of time available, and the skills, experience, and interests of students and the instructor. There are various ways of categorizing these arrangements; Johnson et al. (1991) offer a typology that, though highly abbreviated, suggests a range of formats that can be adapted to large lower-division survey courses.

Formal Learning Teams
Teach specific content: concepts, terms, and skills.

- Plan team activities in detail and provide active and continuous guidance.

- Size, composition, and duration of teams should complement instructional goals.

- The content is taught first to the whole class; team activities emphasize discussion, application, and mastery.

- Monitor performance of the teams; intervene as needed to explain the task or to suggest new ideas and approaches.

- Process issues are reviewed by team members, observed by the instructor, and discussed by the class as a whole.

- The team activity concludes with a formal evaluation. Longer-term team activities include intermediate assessment as well.

Informal Learning Teams

Reinforce instruction, make connections to previous learning, establish a receptive mood for learning, provide opportunities for interaction based on the course content.

- *Narrowly focused team exercises:* Three to five minutes in duration, these are integrated with longer periods of lecture, demonstration, and whole-class discussion. Since the purpose of the team is usually fulfilled within a class period, evaluation and process analysis may not be required.

- *Introductory exercises:* Brief discussions at the beginning of class can be used to engage students' interest in a new topic, review prior knowledge about it, and identify related areas of interest.

- *Transitional exercise:* A quick interlude of small group discussion during the class period can provide smoother transitions from lecture to discussion. Such groups can stimulate participation, identify areas of confusion, and help to raise questions of special interest.

- *Review session:* A few minutes of small group discussion at the end of class can reinforce newly introduced concepts, give students a chance to review and clarify their notes, and encourage them to share impressions of the new concepts and skills that have been presented.

Cooperative Teams

Meet regularly over the course of one or more semesters, support students' long-term development, personalize learning, improve attendance, and provide encouragement and assistance to students in meeting academic demands.

- Teams last an entire semester, a school year, or longer. The goals are stable relationships and continuity of participation.

- Long-term teams may be instituted within a course or by a college, department, or other academic unit.

- Teams should be heterogeneous: diverse in gender, ethnic background, and academic ability.

- Teams should meet regularly and frequently. If they are associated with a course, time for a team meeting should regularly be set aside at the beginning of the class period.

- Teams should be encouraged to deal with both personal and academic issues. They are not focused primarily on specific tasks or projects.

- To ensure clarity of purpose, teams should work from an agenda, provided either by its members or by the instructor.

- The instructor should monitor team performance and intervene if difficulties arise.

All of these groups can be integrated into large lower-division courses, including those based largely on lectures or other forms of conventional instruction. Properly executed, all fulfill the five criteria for successful cooperative learning. Most important, however, all require the instructor to do careful planning. The purpose and goals of the team activity must be clearly explained, and provision must be made to monitor team performance and to intervene if difficulties arise.

Integrating Team Exercises with Other Course Work

For the most part, college-level instruction is not now organized around the principles of cooperative learning. Assignments, textbooks, the examination system, and even the physical arrangements of many large classrooms reflect a more individualistic conception of learning. Under these conditions, how are principles of cooperative learning to be introduced without the appearance of inconsistency?

Instructors who initiate team projects often point out that team activities increase learning. They note that teamwork is widespread in industry and other organizations. Justification along these lines, however, may fail to motivate students because they say little about how teams actually achieve the benefits that are claimed on their behalf, and how a team project complements the content and organization of the specific course in which it is being introduced. This section suggests some ways to supplement the conventional justification for them.

The suggestions are arranged under two headings: rationales for the use of teams in a course or discipline, and the integration of team exercises with other course content. You will note, however, that these categories may overlap in practice.

Rationales for Teams

The following rationales address team exercises as a form of cooperative learning and are thus potentially applicable to a wide range of activities.

Constructivist rationale. Most psychological theory portrays learning as a process of construction (Fosnot, 1996). Students can make sense of a concept only if they build it into the structure of their own prior experience. It is very difficult to create such a structure by oneself, especially in an unfamiliar subject area. Discussion in small groups of peers makes this undertaking much easier.

Linguistic perspective on learning. Scholars of professional language and rhetoric, such as Charles Bazerman (1988, 1991) and James Boyd White (1985), note that when students encounter a discipline or a professional field, they are being exposed to a specialized language. In learning concepts and terms, they are learning to engage in a particular form of discussion. Their grasp of a topic is usually evaluated on the basis of their ability to understand questions about it and to write cogent answers. Students are much more likely to develop this linguistic proficiency if they have both informal and formal opportunities to speak, rather than being restricted to listening and reading.

Tacit dimension of professional and disciplinary knowledge. As Donald Schön has pointed out (1983, 1987), there are many forms of learning that cannot be characterized in terms of propositional knowledge, and thus are not reducible to statements in a textbook or lecture. Practical skills, intuitive judgment, and social context cannot generally be taught by exposition. Some sort of collaborative activity is required. Thus, for example, in a team exercise in a marketing course, students would get a chance to act out the role of a marketing specialist and discover some of the practical exigencies and constraints of the practice of marketing. This background understanding of the social context of marketing would provide a framework within which students may subsequently organize more detailed information of pricing strategy, promotional techniques, and problems of distribution.

Habits and attitudes needed for academic achievement. As Kenneth Bruffee (1999) has pointed out, higher education can be thought of as a form of acculturation. According to this model, becoming successful as a student is a cultural acquisition. Academic competence is not just mastering course content: It also involves the formation of attitudes about schoolwork and the acquisition of habits of regular class attendance, consistent and thorough preparation, and disciplined management of time. Interaction with peers in a classroom can help students learn habits and attitudes needed for academic success more easily. This interaction can be especially helpful for students who come to the United States from other cultures.

Strategies for Integrating Team Exercises

Team exercises provide instructors with feedback mechanisms of unparalleled sensitivity. If teams had no other benefits, they would be justifiable solely on the grounds that they provide detailed information about the success of instruction and bring to light areas of misunderstanding. The following strategies are designed both to take advantage of that feedback and to emphasize its importance to students.

Anticipatory strategies. Formal instruction can be designed to anticipate team exercises. For example, a lecture might introduce a problem or question and review some of the information that could be brought to bear on it. The question or problem could then be posed to teams, who would review their notes and come up with an answer or solution. Alternatively, a lecture could introduce a series of related concepts, and specialized terms and teams convened to explain them and provide illustrations.

Involvement and attention. It is essential that the instructor not be aloof from team exercises. Circulating among the groups, listening, asking questions, and evaluating students' understanding both of concepts and tasks will all help to provide a clearer sense of the students' progress and will also steer them back to the task at hand if they should be inclined to stray from it. The instructor's active attention will emphasize to the students the importance of the team exercise and its connection to other parts of the course.

Short-term adaptation. Information gleaned from the teams can be incorporated into formal lessons. At the start of the next lecture, briefly summarize progress observed in teams, correct specific misconceptions, or highlight unresolved questions that have been raised in the teams.

   Longer-term follow-up activities. Subsequent lectures, discussions, and assignments can be designed to build on the team activities. Teams can report their conclusions in general discussion, a question related to the team activity could be included on the exam, readings related to questions raised by the teams could be assigned.

Establishing a Climate for Supporting Teams

In order for teams to work well, instructors must establish a climate in which students feel comfortable and safe with one another. Faculty must also be prepared to articulate learning and outcome goals, establish timelines, define roles for team members, and provide a framework for the ongoing work of the team. Since many college students do not have solid experience working together in school, cooperative learning provides a fairly structured approach to helping students learn to work together. Johnson et al. (1991) suggest that the instructor's role in establishing a cooperative structure should include five strategies:

- Clearly specify the objectives for the class or project.

- Make decisions about placing students in teams before the lesson or project begins.

- Clearly explain the task and goal structure to the students.

- Monitor the effectiveness of the teams and intervene to provide task assistance (such as answering questions) or to increase students' interpersonal and group skills.

- Evaluate students' achievement and help students discuss how they collaborated with one another.

What are the Social Dynamics of Teams?

The previous sections have covered what might be considered the cognitive aspects of teamwork. There is, however, another dimension of team exercises that should be of concern to you: namely, their social dynamics. Sociologists who have studied teams have identified four distinct stages in the evolution of the team as a social system (Tuckman, 1965; Tuckman & Jensen, 1977). Class activities can be adjusted to accommodate these stages, and if you understand the logic of teams' social evolution, you will be equipped to intervene when things go wrong and the evolution is blocked.

The following description lists the main characteristics of the four stages, and suggests appropriate instructional strategies and techniques.

Stage One: Forming

When a team is first formed, anxiety levels are high. Team members don't know one another and may be uncertain about the purpose and goals of the group; they are often guarded or abrupt in early discussions. The general tasks of the team at this stage are to help members get to know one another, establish trust, and clarify goals. A typical agenda for a meeting might include discussing the goals of the team, narrowing down the focus of the work that is to be undertaken, setting ground rules, agreeing on roles for individual members, and planning subsequent meetings. The "Guidelines for Student Teams" and "Group Exercises" in Part II of this book are useful as teams form.

Instructional strategies. Both the tasks for the team and the rationale for the activity should be clearly stated. A written assignment will provide a useful reference point for team discussions. Goals for the first meeting should be discussed and possibly summarized in the form of a suggested agenda. Procedural suggestions are particularly important. Pointing out the need for team members to get acquainted and build trust in one another may reassure students and diminish anxiety levels. Specific trust-building exercises may be recommended. Concrete suggestions about ground rules and roles will give students a head start on the problems they may be expected to encounter. (For example: Don't come late to meetings, and call member X if you miss class. Roles that should be clearly explained might include archivist, scheduler, and meeting recorder.)

Strategies for intervention. Sit in on meetings. Ask questions to verify progress. Draw out reticent team members. Probe students' interests and areas of expertise. Invite students to ask questions to clarify the task. Ask what procedural rules the team has adopted and how they've focused their work. Assess the realism of their responses. After the team exercise ends, share general impressions of the progress made by the teams. Point out problems and invite suggested solutions.

Stage Two: Storming

Even in the most successful teams, disagreements and conflicts develop. Characteristic incidents include expression of hostility among team members, formation of cliques, challenges to or criticism of other team members, disputes about leadership, or violation of team norms (missing meetings or failing to carry out agreed-upon tasks, for example). Expressions of dissatisfaction are often ambiguous, involving both personal grievance and concern about overall team performance and a member's contribution to it. The team can transcend the conflict by focusing on the performance aspect. Conflict can be used to stimulate ideas about how the team can function more efficiently. Characteristic tasks at this stage include reexamining the interests and abilities of a member who isn't contributing and modifying that person's role if necessary; rotating leadership or encouraging the present leadership to adopt a new style or different procedures; reevaluating roles, ground rules, and work plans. The section on "Managing Conflict" in Part II has ideas and exercises that are helpful in this stage.

Instructional strategies. Discuss conflict and its significance in the evolution of teams. Suggest strategies for resolving disagreements. Encourage team members to articulate their differences. Model and encourage active listening. Give examples of how dissatisfaction might be expressed ambiguously, and encourage students to reformulate these complaints so that they focus on performance. Ask for written reports on group process that focus specifically on differences and how they are resolved.

Strategies for intervention. Sit in with teams that are having difficulty. Articulate disagreements if students are having difficulty doing so on their own. Model constructive complaints and positive responses. Simulate problem solving. Solicit the participation of all members. Ask team members to spell out and reevaluate norms and procedures. Make specific suggestions to improve efficiency.

Stage Three: Norming

Mutual expectations of team members are understood more clearly. Individual members feel pressure to accept decisions, defer to leadership, and commit time and energy to the team enterprise. The characteristic task at this stage is balancing and coordination of individual contributions. Typical problems include encouraging and coordinating diverse contributions, identifying upper and lower bounds of individual commitment to the group, and deciding how to share information and how to meld individual contributions into a group effort. The role of the team leader is more important than ever, but by now all members of the group should take responsibility for improving cooperation. As the team settles down to a working group, the "Team Evaluation" section in Part II provides ideas for monitoring teamwork and evaluating the process.

Instruction and intervention. Teams that have reached this stage are more self-sufficient, and one's role as instructor is diminished accordingly. If the quality of the final work product is at issue, it may be useful to discuss criteria for evaluation. Teams can be encouraged to share in the responsibility of evaluation; the instructor can suggest guidelines for criticism and model constructive responses to other members' work. Assessment of group process should shift focus, concentrating now on procedures for coordinating the work product and balancing contributions of individual members.

Stage Four: Performing
The team has overcome uncertainty and conflict and can now function as an integrated unit. Confident of their teammates' support, individual members perform their tasks enthusiastically and are able to take risks and exercise imagination. Everyone feels responsible for the work of the whole group. Members are committed to each other's success, and willingly help, coach, and advise one another. The team should now be looking for new challenges: improving the final product of their work, fine-tuning group processes, drawing on new resources from outside the team, looking for areas in which members might make new contributions.

Instructional strategies. The students now require very little guidance. You serve mainly as a resource, providing ideas, contacts, references, and logistical support. If there is a final work product or assignment, suggestions for quality control may be in order. Opportunities for teams to reflect on their achievements should be provided. Assessments of team performance by individual members should also be solicited. Asking teams to evaluate the work of other teams can offer new perspectives on their own work. You may also ask students to reflect in writing about what they have learned from the team exercise, whether it helped them understand course material and increased their sense of investment and participation in the course. The results of this assessment may be impressionistic but will nonetheless provide crucial data for deciding whether to repeat the team exercise when the course is offered next, and if so, whether and how it should be modified.

Summing Up
The specific stages and strategies identified by this model are perhaps less significant than some of the more general conclusions that can be drawn from it.

- First, the instructor and his or her students should bear in mind that the formation of teams is a developmental process. Conflict and tension are signs of progress, not failure. "Storming" is counterproductive only if team members are unable to resolve their difficulties and move on to the next stage. Techniques of conflict management may prove useful in such cases. They can be implemented either by the instructor or by one or more team members acting on their own.

- Second, teams are more likely to progress through the stages if members are open with one another, if challenges are clearly articulated, and if issues of group process are thoroughly discussed and examined. Faculty can help bring about an atmosphere of openness and reason, but success in this area ultimately depends on the good faith of individual team members.

- Third, the psychological dynamics of teams are significantly influenced by the clarity with which goals, procedures, and expectations are articulated. These aspects of the team exercise depend primarily on the instructor's initiative. The insight and diligence of the team members obviously help, but there is no substitute for well-thought-out exercises and procedures.

- The general lesson of the developmental model is that where difficulties in group processes persist, the instructor can and should intervene, but the guidance one can provide amounts to a more explicit and self-conscious enactment of functions one hopes students eventually will learn to fulfill on their own.

How is Teamwork Evaluated?

One of the most frequently discussed aspects of teamwork is team evaluation. Both instructors and students have concerns about the best ways for evaluating teamwork. How does one evaluate the work that a team has done?

Students must know in advance that performance will be evaluated individually as well as collectively (Meyers & Jones, 1993). They must see the results of the assessment and know what consequences are likely given varying levels of performance. Team members must know that they cannot let other team members do all the work while they do nothing. To alleviate such concerns, team members should have the opportunity to evaluate their peers when completing a team project (Part II contains a sample "Team Member Peer Evaluation" form).

Instructors should have the teamwork evaluation plan in place as the project begins, so that students know from the onset of the project how they will be evaluated. Johnson et al. (1991) suggest the following strategies to ensure timely, accurate, and effective assessments.

- Design writing assignments, reviews, and other forms of evaluation, some of which occur early enough in the course to influence subsequent performance and affect group process.

- Assessment tools can include individual tests for all students, team papers or presentations, observations of a team meeting by the instructor, or a review of the work of one student selected at random to represent the progress of the team.

- Students should be encouraged to reflect on the results of the assessment and use them to improve team process. Set aside time for this reflection, discuss fair ways to share information, and suggest how it might be interpreted and used as a guide for action.

Conclusion

Despite its recent popularity, teamwork remains an extremely recent development in American higher education. Not surprisingly, this innovation has led to many misconceptions about the nature of cooperative learning. Team exercises require at least as much preparation as an average lecture, and they require much of your attention even when the students are actually convened in their teams. Team exercises present problems of management and evaluation that are complex but not mysterious or unsolvable. Used judiciously, teams can effectively supplement conventional instruction, increase student satisfaction, and improve students' grasp of content.

References

Astin, A. (1993). *What matters in college: Four critical years revisited.* San Francisco, CA: Jossey-Bass.

Bazerman, C. (1988). *Shaping written knowledge: The genre and activity of the experimental article in science.* Madison, WI: University of Wisconsin Press.

Bazerman, C. (Ed.). (1991). *Textual dynamics of the professions: Historical and contemporary studies of writing in professional communities.* Madison, WI: University of Wisconsin Press.

Bruffee, K. A. (1999). *Collaborative learning: Higher education, interdependence, and the authority of knowledge.* Baltimore, MD: Johns Hopkins University Press.

Cooper, J., et al. (1990). *Cooperative learning and college instruction: Effective use of student learning teams.* Long Beach, CA: University Academic Publications Program.

Cuseo, J. B. (1991). *The freshman orientation seminar: A research-based rationale for its value, delivery, and content.* (The Freshman Year Experience Monograph Series No. 4). University of South Carolina, National Resource Center for the Freshman Year Experience.

Davis, B. G. (1993). *Tools for teaching.* San Francisco, CA: Jossey-Bass.

Fosnot, C. T. (Ed.). (1996). *Constructivism: Theory, perspectives, and practice.* New York, NY: Teachers College Press.

Frierson, H. T. (1986). Two intervention methods: Effects on groups of predominantly black nursing students' board scores. *Journal of Research and Development in Education, 19,* 18–23.

Gabelnick, F., MacGregor, J., Matthews, R. S., & Smith, B. L. (1992). Learning communities and general education. *Perspectives, 22* (1).

Graves, N., & Graves, T. (1989). Should we teach cooperative skills as a part of each cooperative lesson? *Cooperative Learning, 10* (2), 19–20.

Hill, P. J. (1985). *The rationale for learning communities.* Paper presented at the Inaugural Conference of the Washington Center for Improving the Quality of Undergraduate Education, Olympia, WA.

Johnson, D. W., Johnson, R. T., & Smith, K. A. (1991). *Cooperative learning: Increasing college faculty instructional productivity.* Washington, DC: The George Washington University, School of Education and Human Development. (ASHE-ERIC Higher Education Report No. 4)

Johnson, D. W., Johnson, R. T., & Smith, K. A. (1998, July/August). Cooperative learning returns to college: What evidence is there that it works? *Change, 30* (4), 26–35.

Meyers, C., & Jones, T. B. (1993). *Promoting active learning strategies for the college classroom.* San Francisco, CA: Jossey-Bass.

Schön, D. A. (1983). *The reflective practitioner: How professionals think in action.* New York, NY: Basic Books.

Schön, D. A. (1987). *Educating the reflective practitioner: Toward a new design for teaching and learning in the professions.* San Francisco, CA: Jossey-Bass.

Sharan, S., & Sharan, Y. (1992). *Expanding cooperative learning through group investigation.* New York, NY: Teachers College Press.

Slavin, R. (1995). *Cooperative learning: Theory, research, and practice.* Boston, MA: Allyn and Bacon.

Smith, B. L. (1991). Taking structure seriously: The learning community model. *Liberal Education, 77* (2), 42–48.

Tinto, V., & Riemer, S. (1998). From material prepared for a presentation at the Conference on Replacing Remediation in Higher Education at Stanford University, January 26–27, 1998, sponsored by the Ford Foundation and the United States Department of Education.

Treisman, P. U. (1983). Improving the performance of minority students in college-level mathematics. *Innovation Abstracts, 5* (17).

Tuckman, B. (1965). Developmental sequence in small groups. *Psychological Bulletin, 61* (6), 384–399.

Tuckman, B., & Jensen, M. A. C. (1977). Stages of small-group development revisited. *Group and Organizational Studies, 2* (4), 419–427.

White, J. B. (1985). *Heracles' bow: Essays on the rhetoric and poetics of the law.* Madison, WI: University of Wisconsin Press.

II PART

Building
Effective Teams

2

Technology and Teamwork

Laptops, client-server technology, networked residence halls, computer labs, computerized classrooms, high-speed Internet connections... Whenever these technologies appear on college campuses, they create opportunities for new forms of teamwork. If students can meet electronically, they never need to arrange a plan to meet outside of the classroom in which the course meets. If they have space on a web server, they can view team members' work instantly—not just text, but sound, video, graphics, any format they are working in. File formats not supported by browsers can be downloaded and run on specialized software.

With email, chatroom, and listserv technology, teams can discuss problems online. They can supplement their planning process electronically, linking to the instructor without having to inquire about office hours, to the library without having to cross campus, to classmates without having to track them down in their residence halls.

If suitable infrastructure is in place, students can present, submit, or distribute their work electronically, eliminating delays, printer crises, and copying costs. The instructor, if she chooses, can respond through the same medium, selecting from a variety of styles to match the purpose and content of her response. She can produce a running commentary in a text document, add oral comments as sound clips, intervene in email discussions if she is included in the address list, and review and evaluate an electronic archive documenting group interaction.

How Do These Resources Enhance the Functions of Teams?

These are communication technologies. Their effect is felt primarily on interactions within the team and between the team and those outside—classmates, instructor, and support personnel. Many of their effects are beneficial, but there are costs as well. Let us examine these effects, to see how an instructor might exploit their benefits, while reducing the costs as much as possible.

Instantaneity

The time required for communication telescopes dramatically. Hit the send button and the email message appears in all members' inboxes. Click the link on the browser bar and the latest draft of the paper appears within a few seconds.

Benefits: Easier and more frequent interaction. Less frustration. Less waiting. Less down time.

Costs: Too much speed can lead to superficiality. Students need time for thought and reflection.

Strategies: Ask students to spend time away from the computer, processing electronic output. Have them turn in hard copy with mechanical annotations corresponding to different stages of the project.

Require submission of handwritten material: notes, brainstorming, outlines, agendas for team meetings.

Assign extended analytical pieces: problem statements, explanations of design proposal, reflections on team process, or detailed responses to the work of other team members.

Precision

Team members respond to one another's precise words, not to a general impression or a vague recollection of what they said. Email and chatrooms encourage brief, focused messages. It is easier to see where a discussion gets off topic. Data—drawing, comments, plans, or discussions—are reproduced byte-by-byte. If equipment is working properly, nothing is lost in storage or transmission.

Benefits: Inaccuracy is reduced, confusion is avoided. It is easier for teammates to evaluate each other's work, criticism, or suggestions.

Costs: Nuance is lost. Emotional context is lost. Students communicating electronically cannot access tone, inflection, or body language. Work products are more vulnerable. Months of work can be wiped out by a system crash or hardware failure.

Strategies: Require periodic face-to-face meetings. Encourage or require written or oral reflection on email exchanges. Ask students to identify areas of misunderstanding and blocked communication.

> **Establish guidelines for backing up work.** Make space on a server available for team archives. For long projects, require periodic deposit of archives with the instructor. Require printouts of essential work products.

Documentation

Electronic communications require that thought, planning, and discussion be reduced to a format that is easily stored. If students are required to save all team products, they can very quickly accumulate an archive with sequential drafts of work products, resources used, process records of planning and discussion, and comprehensive records of individual contributions to the total group effort.

Benefits: Large-scale archives are an important resource for process analysis by students and instructor. They aid evaluation of individual contribution, both by the student and the instructor.

On a smaller scale, archives allow quick recovery of earlier plans or drafts, easy comparison of different versions of a work product, quick reviews of plans and decisions.

Costs: Quantity does not guarantee quality. Drafts with small changes can accumulate quickly. A very large, heterogeneous archive can overwhelm users with data.

Strategies: Require students to process archives before submitting them. They can be asked to sort through the data and select what is most significant. They can be asked to provide annotations. They can be assigned to synthesize and reflect on archival data.

Workforce Preparations

Some professional fields already require extensive use of electronic resources. Deploying those resources in an instructional context helps to prepare students for their responsibilities in the work place.

Benefits: Students learn specific technologies. They also learn problem solving strategies: what to do when equipment malfunctions, how to bring a team member up to speed on a new piece of software, how to coordinate efforts in an electronic environment, how to exploit institutional resources and work around resource deficiencies.

Costs: Time spent learning and problem solving may detract from learning the content that the team project is designed to teach. System failure or lack of access to hardware and software may block team efforts and enormously increase workload. If not all students have access to and sufficient knowledge of hardware and software, some may be left out and receive fewer of the benefits the team project is designed to produce.

Strategies: Evaluate resources well in advance of implementing the team project. Do all the students already own or have access to the required hardware and software? How many of the required items do they already use, and how readily will they learn to handle those they have not used? How reliable are the systems that the institution provides, and how extensive is the support available to students?

Do a dry run of critical elements of the team project. Use all the resources the students may have to use—a laptop that lacks the appropriate software, a telephone line with a slow modem, the oldest computer cluster on campus. Where multiple platforms or versions of software exist, create test files to check compatibility.

Assign volunteers to run a pilot version of the electronic team project during the semester before implementation. Have the team keep a problem log.

Have graduate assistants run the project or serve as consultants and troubleshooters for the pilot version and compile a searchable help file with a topic index, frequently asked questions, and links to resources.

Ask students to evaluate the project, describe problems they have encountered, and suggest changes. Identify the problems that are most time consuming or have interfered most with student learning, and redesign the project to reduce or eliminate them.

3

Exercise for Students: How Do I Learn Best?

VARK Inventory

Note: *An interesting exercise that students can do on their own (or on the Internet) to learn about their preferred learning styles.*

The VARK inventory is a questionnaire that aims to find out something about your preferences for the way you work with information. You will have a preferred learning style, and one part of that learning style is your preference for the intake and output of ideas and information. For more detailed information about scoring VARK, for doing VARK online, and for study practices keyed to VARK preferences, go to http://www.active-learning-site.com/.

Directions
Choose the answer that best explains your preference. Please select more than one response if a single answer does not match your perception. Leave blank any question that does not apply.

1. You are about to give directions to a person who is standing with you. She is staying in a hotel in town and wants to visit your house later. She has a rental car. Would you:

   a) draw a map on paper

   b) tell her the directions

   c) write down the directions (without a map)

   d) pick her up from her hotel in your car

2. You are not sure whether a word should be spelled 'dependent' or 'dependant.' Do you:

   c) look it up in the dictionary

a) see the word in your mind and choose by the way it looks

b) sound it out in your mind

d) write both versions down on paper and choose one

3. You have just received a copy of your itinerary for a world trip. This is of interest to a friend. Would you:

b) phone her immediately and tell her about it

c) send her a copy of the printed itinerary

a) show her on a map of the world

d) share what you plan to do at each place you visit

4. You are going to cook something as a special treat for your family. Do you:

d) cook something familiar without need for instructions

a) thumb through the cookbook looking for ideas from the pictures

c) refer to a specific cookbook where there is a recipe you know about

5. A group of tourists have been assigned to you to learn about wildlife reserves or parks. Would you:

d) drive them to a wildlife reserve or park

a) show them slides and photographs

c) give them pamphlets or a book on wildlife reserves or parks

b) drive them to a national park

6. You are about to purchase a new stereo. Other than price, what would most influence your decision?

b) the salesperson telling you what you want to know

c) reading the details about it

d) playing with the controls and listening to it

a) it looks really smart and fashionable

7. Recall a time in your life when you learned how to do something like playing a new board game. Try to avoid using a very physical skill (e.g., riding a bike). How did you learn best? By

   a) visual clues—pictures, diagrams, charts

   c) written instructions

   b) listening to somebody explaining it

   d) doing it or trying it

8. You have an eye problem. Would you prefer that the doctor:

   b) tell you what is wrong

   a) show you a diagram of what is wrong

   d) use a model to show you what is wrong

9. You are about to learn to use a new program on a computer. Would you:

   d) sit down at the keyboard and begin to experiment with the program's features

   c) read the manual that comes with the program

   b) telephone a friend and ask questions about it

10. You are staying in a hotel and have a rental car. You would like to visit friends whose address/location you do not know. Would you like them to:

    a) draw you a map on paper

    b) tell you the directions

    c) write down the directions (without a map)

    d) collect you from the hotel in their car

11. Apart from price, what would most influence your decision to buy a particular textbook?

    d) you have used a copy before

    b) a friend talking about it

    c) quickly reading parts of it

    a) the way it looks is appealing

12. A new movie has arrived in town. What would most influence your decision to go (or not go)?

   b) you heard a radio review about it

   c) you read a review about it

   a) you saw a preview of it

13. Do you prefer a lecturer or teacher who likes to use:

   c) textbooks, handouts, readings

   a) flow diagrams, charts, slides

   d) field trips, labs, practical sessions

   b) discussion, guest speakers

Total from these pages   A: **Visual**   _____

                                   B: **Aural**   _____

                                   C: **Read**/Write   _____

                                   D: **Kinesthetic**   _____

V

If you have a strong preference for **Visual** learning, you should use some or all of the following:

INTAKE—To take in information, use

- underlining
- different colors
- highlighters
- symbols
- flow charts
- charts
- graphs
- pictures, videos, posters, slides
- different spatial arrangements on the page
- white space
- textbooks with diagrams, pictures
- lecturers who use gestures and picturesque language

STUDYING—To create an effective and learnable package

Convert your lecture notes into a learnable package by reducing them into page pictures by trying the following:

- Reconstruct the images in different ways—try different spatial arrangements.
- Redraw your pages from memory.
- Replace words with symbols or initials.
- Look at your pages.

OUTPUT—To perform well in an examination

- Recall the "pictures" of pages.
- Draw—use diagrams where appropriate.
- Write exam answers.
- Practice turning your visuals back into words.

You are holistic rather than reductionist in your approach. You want the whole picture. Visual learners do not like handouts, words, lectures, textbooks, or assessments that are based on word usage, syntax, and grammar. You are going to watch TV.

A

If you have a strong preference for learning by **A**ural method (hearing), you should use some or all of the following:

INTAKE—To take in information

- Attend lectures.
- Attend tutorials.
- Discuss topics with other students.
- Discuss topics with your lecturers.
- Explain new ideas to other people.
- Use a tape recorder.
- Remember the interesting examples, stories, jokes.
- Describe the overheads, pictures, and other visuals to somebody who was not there.
- Leave spaces in your lecture notes for later recall.

STUDYING—To create an effective and learnable package

Convert your lecture notes into a learnable package by reducing them to only one page for every three by trying the following:

- Your lecture notes may be poor because you prefer to listen. You will need to expand your notes by talking with others and collecting notes from the textbook.
- Put your summarized notes onto tapes and listen to them.
- Ask others to "hear" your understanding of a topic.
- Read your summarized notes out loud.
- Explain your notes to another aural person.

OUTPUT—To perform well in an examination

- Talk with the faculty member.
- Listen to your tapes and write ideas down.
- Spend time in quiet places recalling the ideas.
- Practice writing answers to old exam questions.
- Speak your answers.

You prefer to have all of this page explained to you. The written words are not as valuable as those you hear. You will probably go and tell somebody about this.

R

If you have a strong preference for learning by **R**eading and Writing, you should use some or all of the following:

INTAKE—To take in information, use

- lists
- headings
- dictionaries
- glossaries
- handouts
- textbooks
- reading—library
- lecture notes (verbatim)
- lecturers who use words well and have lots of information in sentences and notes
- essays
- manuals (computing and laboratory)

STUDYING—To create an effective and learnable package

Convert your lecture notes into a learnable package by reducing them to only one page for every three by trying the following:

- Write out the words again and again.
- Read your notes (silently) again and again.
- Rewrite the ideas and principles into other words.
- Organize any diagrams and graphs into statements, i.e., "The trend is..."
- Imagine your lists arranged in multiple choice style and determine a variety of questions.

OUTPUT—To perform well in an examination

- Write exam answers.
- Practice with multiple choice questions.
- Write paragraphs, beginnings, endings.
- Write your lists (a, b, c, d; 1, 2, 3, 4).
- Arrange your words into main points or by importance.

You like this page because the emphasis is on words and lists. You believe the meanings are within the words, so the talk was OK, but this handout is better. You are heading for the library.

K

If you have a strong preference for **K**inesthetic (doing) learning, you should use some or all of the following:

INTAKE—To take in information, use

- your senses—sight, touch, taste, smell, hearing
- laboratories
- field trips
- field tours
- examples of principles
- lecturers who give real-life examples
- applications
- hands-on approaches (computing)
- trial and error
- exhibits, samples, photographs
- recipes—solutions to problems
- previous exam papers

STUDYING—To create an effective and learnable package

Convert your lecture notes into a learnable package by reducing them to only one page for every three by trying the following:

- Your lecture notes may be poor because the topics were not concrete or relevant.
- You will remember the "real" things that happened.
- Put plenty of examples into your summary. Use case studies and applications to help with principles and abstract concepts.
- Talk about your notes with another kinesthetic person.
- Use pictures and photographs that illustrate an idea.
- Go back to the laboratory or your lab manual.
- Recall the experiments, field trips.

OUTPUT—To perform well in an examination

- Write practice answers or paragraphs.
- Role play the exam situation in your own room.

You want to experience the exam so that you can understand it. The ideas on this page are only valuable if they sound practical, real, and relevant to you. You need to do things in order to understand.

4

Guidelines for Student Teams

Use "Guidelines for Student Teams" as a handout to give student teams some direction and basic information as they start their work.

During the course of the semester, you will be meeting with your team at least weekly. At these weekly meetings you should, at minimum, share the results of the research that each team member has done during that week, review upcoming assignments, and check your team project progress against your project plan to make sure that you are on schedule. As the semester progresses, you will probably need to meet more frequently to work on specific team project assignments. Team meetings, depending on how the team conducts itself, may be very productive or very frustrating. While there are no hard and fast rules, and you will need to discover what works best for your team, the following are some general guidelines to follow in order to maximize productivity and minimize frustration.

These guidelines cover two subjects: 1) certain specialized roles that need to be assigned for each meeting and 2) team meetings themselves. The roles that need to be assigned are coordinator, timekeeper/recorder, and facilitator. Team meetings can be divided into three segments: preparing for the meeting, conducting the meeting, and what happens between meetings.

Specialized Roles

The roles of coordinator, timekeeper/recorder, and facilitator should be assigned for each meeting and are in addition to the normal team roles that each person plays. It is very important that these roles be rotated among team members. Note that an assigned leader is not one of the specialized roles. Teams do need effective leadership, but they do not need a leader. It is best if the leaders (note that this is "leaders," not "leader") emerge from the team's interaction and change over time.

Coordinator. The responsibilities of the coordinator are to schedule the meeting and to manage the meeting. These responsibilities are discussed in more detail in the next section.

Timekeeper/recorder. The responsibilities of the timekeeper/recorder are to make sure that the team stays within agreed upon time frames and to keep a record of the meeting. These responsibilities are also discussed in more detail in the next section.

Facilitator. A team facilitator will be assigned to each team and must be included in the team's required weekly meeting. (The team can decide whether or not to invite the facilitator to additional meetings.) It is the responsibility of the facilitator to observe and give the team feedback on its process so that it can improve its functioning as a team. The team facilitator does not provide substantive help on the team project itself.

Team Meetings

Preparing to Meet

Preparation is very important to the success of meetings. For your regularly scheduled weekly meeting, the coordinator makes sure that everyone remembers where and when the meeting is to take place, especially early in the semester before the weekly meeting becomes second nature to you. Later in the semester, when you add meetings to your schedule, the coordinator for each meeting establishes the place and time (starting and ending) of the meeting, in consultation with team members. The coordinator reviews the agenda created collaboratively by the team at the end of the previous meeting and informs the team of any necessary adjustments. The participants confirm their attendance and do any required homework.

Meeting

Managing the Meeting

The coordinator starts the meeting on time and makes every effort to follow the agenda. The coordinator performs the gatekeeping function, making sure that everyone has a chance to participate and that no one consumes all the air time. The coordinator manages conflicts and tries to bring the team to consensus. Near the end of the meeting, the coordinator clarifies actions that need to be taken.

Team Members' Responsibilities

Team members arrive on time and actively participate in the meeting. They both give and seek information. They listen actively, give effective interpersonal feedback, are supportive, and disagree in constructive ways.

Keeping a Record

The timekeeper/recorder is the official clock-watcher (and should be the only one). He or she sees to it that the team stays within agreed upon time frames, and informs members of elapsed time and time remaining in the meeting. The timekeeper/recorder is responsible for keeping a record of the meeting, including a summary of the discussion, decisions that were made, and areas of remaining disagreement. Near the end of the meeting, the recorder summarizes the meeting and notes future actions required by members. The team assigns coordinator and timekeeper/recorder roles for the next meeting. The team formulates an agenda for the next meeting.

Creating an Agenda

Creating an agenda is an important activity: An agenda that is too structured can stifle creativity and openness, while an agenda that is not structured enough can fail to provide sufficient guidance for the meeting. Here are some tips for planning an agenda.

- Write down the major items that the team wants to tackle.

- Ensure that all team members have the opportunity to contribute.

- Clarify what the team wants to accomplish for each item—discussion, brainstorming, making a decision, taking action, etc.

- Prioritize items and allocate time to each.

Paying Attention to Team Dynamics

As the last exercise at each meeting, the team focuses on its own dynamics. An essential component in a team's success is its ability to grow and learn from its experiences. Growth includes building additional skills, an increased ability to function in the roles required by the team's tasks, and the willingness and ability to build a climate that encourages change and learning. A team's ability to be flexible and to learn about its own strengths and weaknesses is essential to keeping energy and motivation high and to achieving high performance results.

Between Meetings

- The coordinator for the next meeting refines the tentative agenda agreed upon at the last meeting and distributes it to all members of the team and the team facilitator with a reminder about day, time, and location for the next meeting.

- The recorder prepares the "Team Meeting Report" form, distributes it to all team members, and submits it to the section leader.

- Each member of the team meets all deadlines for completing the work for which he or she agreed to be responsible.

Two Important Tools for Team Learning

Assessment

The first important tool for team learning is assessment. Two types of assessment should be used—self-assessment and team assessment. Each team member assesses her or his own behavior during team meetings by filling out, before each meeting is adjourned, the "Team Meeting Self-Analysis" form. This form is for the team member's own use in monitoring her or his team skills. Team assessment happens in several ways. One way is through the observations of the team facilitator. The team facilitator will share her or his observations about the team at the end of the weekly team meeting. After the team facilitator has shared these observations, the team discusses how they worked together and establishes objectives for improving their effectiveness. Another way in which the team assesses its performance is through the "Team Member Reaction" form. This form will be completed and submitted to your section leader periodically throughout the semester. Your section leader will provide you with a summary of the evaluations to use as a basis for discussing and improving your team process.

Feedback

The second important tool for team learning is feedback. Feedback is a nonjudgmental observation that describes a problem and how it affects another team member or the team. Most people at first find it difficult to give feedback. And sometimes people do take negative feedback personally or get angry. Giving feedback, however, becomes easier with practice and is essential for good communication—it should become part of the whole team's way of dealing with issues. In giving feedback, describe the problem and how it affects you and the team. State how you feel and describe what you would like instead. Here are four hints for success.

- Be specific, not general.

- Describe behavior rather than judging the person.

- To avoid blaming, start with the word "I," not the word "you."

- Be timely.

Learning to give effective feedback is an important aspect of teamwork; it is well worth the effort that it takes to become proficient.

5

Group Exercises

The Egg Drop: A Team-Building Activity

The Egg Drop activity is an exercise that instructors can use early in the semester. Team members quickly become acquainted. The activity helps to bond team members and to build team spirit.

Many organizations are using shootouts to encourage teamwork and creativity. In a shootout, a number of teams are given the same assignment—for example, coming up with a new product. A public competition is then staged in order to select the best new product idea. The egg drop exercise is a simulation of this process.

Mission
Your team has 30 minutes to design and build a new product to catch a raw egg without it breaking when dropped from chin level by a team member. The only resources available to you are 18 plastic straws and 30 inches of masking tape; no other materials may be used. In addition to building the product, your team is to write a 30-second advertising spot for the product.

Procedure
Each team will independently build an egg catcher using the available resources. The egg catcher must be transportable and may not be fixed to the floor or any other surface during the shootout. After 30 minutes, teams will assemble for the shootout. Each team will be asked to deliver its 30-second advertising spot, and then one team member will drop the egg.

Selection of Winner
The following criteria will be used to determine the winner of the egg drop:

1. Did the egg catcher catch the egg without breaking? (To be considered a catch, the egg must not roll off onto the floor.)

2. If more than one egg catcher catches the egg without breaking, which one used the fewest resources? (For this calculation, 3 inches of tape equals 1 straw.)

3. If a tie exists after criteria 1 and 2 have been applied, which advertising spot was more persuasive? (This determination is to be made by the section leader.)

Tower-Building Exercise: A Team-Building Activity

The Tower-Building Exercise is another activity to use early in the semester. Through the exercise team members quickly become acquainted. The activity also helps to bond team members and to build team spirit. The exercise includes a set of follow-up discussion questions.

Objective
To study team dynamics in a performance-based situation.

Procedure

1. Each person will bring materials to class for building a tower; these must fit into a shoebox. No preconstruction is allowed. Bring only raw materials.

2. In class, each team will build a tower. Be sure to label your tower with a team name. After the towers are completed, the towers will be judged on the basis of the following:

   • Height

   • Stability

   • Beauty

   • Meaning

3. Representatives from each team will present the tower to the rest of the class and describe the meaning of their tower. Teams will inspect other towers, and all individuals will rate towers other than their own.

4. The team with the winning tower will receive a prize.

Discussion Questions

1. In what way did your team's tower represent the culture and norms of your team?

2. What problems arose in the building of your team's tower? How were these problems resolved?

3. Was there any team conflict either in the planning or the building stages of the tower exercise? Briefly explain. How was the conflict resolved?

4. Were any team strengths revealed as a result of doing the tower exercise? Any team weaknesses? Explain.

5. How cohesive were you as a team by the end of the tower exercise? Explain.

6. How do you feel about the functioning of your team as a whole?

7. Are you able to recognize any team members who have strengths in special knowledge/skills?

8. How do you feel about your personal contribution/performance to the teamwork?

9. What special knowledge/skills do you feel you can contribute to help the team?

10. Do you think you will be able to work well with this team for the rest of the year? (Elaborate on your answer.)

Jot down and discuss questions 1-9 with your team members. If time permits, we will have you share some of the details about your team dynamics and performance with the rest of the class.

Type up and hand in question 10 for next time.

Straw Exercise: A Team-Building Activity

The Straw Exercise is another variation of a team-building activity to help team members become acquainted. It includes two self-assessment exercises that can be adapted to any of the team-building exercises.

Your Team's Challenge

Design the world's tallest straw structure. Your team will be given a number of drinking straws and one roll of masking tape. Your challenge is to work as a team to design and construct, in the time permitted, the tallest structure possible using the tape and straws. Just to make it a little more challenging, your creation must be freestanding: It cannot be taped to the floor, ceiling, or a piece of furniture. Your team will have ten minutes to plan and create a structure. Following the activity, each team will briefly explain the features of their construction—please choose a spokesperson for your team.

Follow-up Assignment

Complete exercises 1 and 2 on the following pages individually; then meet as a team to discuss how your team worked and write a one paragraph team profile.

Exercises 1 and 2 can be used as teamwork self-assessment exercises.

Name _____ Section _____

Exercise 1

To be completed before discussing the Straw Exercise with other members of your team.

Think about how your team interacted while completing the construction project; then answer the following questions. When possible, name the person(s) who took various roles.

1. What did your team do immediately after receiving the assignment?

2. Did your team organize the task? If so, how?

3. Describe the specific roles (e.g., tape cutter, builder, etc.) that each team member took and how these roles were decided.

4. Which aspects of the construction project did your team complete most successfully?

5. Which aspects might your team change next time?

Name _____ Section _____

Exercise 2

To be completed before discussing the Straw Exercise with other members of your team.

In the previous exercise, you identified the specific roles you and your team members took while completing the construction project. The chart below lists general roles that are applicable to team projects. Complete each column by placing a check mark next to any of the roles pertinent to you. You may have multiple check marks in a column. If you are not sure about a particular role, use a question mark instead of a check mark.

Possible roles	*Roles that I took for the project*	*Roles that I have taken in the past*	*Roles that I am most comfortable taking*
Organizer			
Leader			
Manager			
Initiator			
Follower			
Conciliator			
Presenter			
Creator			
Ideator			
Timekeeper			
Equal participant			
Nonparticipant			
Assistant			
Observer			
Others (please indicate)			

Team Charter Assignment

Note: There are three parts to this assignment. Please be sure to complete all of them.

Getting Started: Developing Ground Rules

Anyone who plays sports has to learn the rules. Anyone who learns to play an instrument has to learn the techniques. The rules of "how we do things here" (the etiquette of the situation, the appropriate behaviors) are the ground rules.

Teams often begin making assumptions about ground rules. Members believe that everyone knows how it should be and how everyone should behave. When someone else's behavior fails to conform to one's own expectations, people tend to be surprised. Even more importantly, because the rules are not clear and because there has been no discussion as to how problems will be managed, unnecessary conflict follows.

There are many ground rules that effective teams must address. There is a great deal of freedom and latitude for team members to decide how they want to work together and what they will do when their process is not working, but those decisions must be made and the team must work together to make them.

Some of the important procedural issues that must be decided are listed below, with some examples of the kinds of questions that might be addressed. Use these as a starting point to develop this section of your team charter.

Attendance

- Other than our weekly meetings, how often should we meet?

- How long should our meetings be?

- When is it OK to miss a meeting?

- How do we inform each other when we can't be there?

Lateness

- Since team meetings should start on time, how do we deal with lateness?

- What does "on time" mean?

Interruptions

- How do we deal with interruptions?
- What is allowed? phone calls? messages?

Food/coffee/breaks

- Do we have food, coffee?
- Who cleans up?
- How many breaks should we have?

Participation

- What do we mean by participation?
- How do we encourage participation?
- Are there group norms that we can establish to encourage participation?

Norms

- What behaviors are permissible?
- How do we deal with inappropriate humor?
- How do we deal with people who dominate, resist, are too quiet or noisy, etc.?
- How will we monitor our process and progress?

Decision making

- How do we make decisions?
- What decisions must be agreed to by all?
- What does consensus mean?

Quality of work

- What do we mean by quality?
- How do we encourage quality?
- Are there group norms that we can establish to encourage quality?

- What will we do if a group member's work doesn't meet our quality standards?

Information sharing

- How are we going to share information?

Other

- Are there other issues that have a positive or negative impact on our team?

The Next Step: Addressing Some Fundamental Issues

The process of developing ground rules for "how we do things" should raise some other, more fundamental issues that every group must face when it is in the process of becoming a team. These issues need to be addressed early in a group's life and continuously revisited during the team's life. In this section of your team charter, try to answer the question posed about each issue. Expect that you will need to return to a discussion of one or more of these issues more than once during the semester.

A. Goal Issues (What is the team trying to accomplish?)
   To be an effectively functioning team, individual members must have a shared, agreed-upon, common definition of the team's mission—its reason for existence as a team. Goal conflicts must be recognized and clearly resolved. Periodically review the objectives of this semester's team project and check in with each other to make sure that you have a shared definition of your goals.

B. Role Issues (Who should be doing what to help the team reach its goals?)
   One particular source of problems on a team is role ambiguity: Members are simply not clear about what they expect of one another. In addition to the problem of role ambiguity, there are two forms of role conflict that are frequently observed in teams. First, self-other conflicts arise because what someone else expects of a team member does not fit the expectations of that team member. Second, other-other conflicts arise when two or more team members have expectations of a group member that, although they are unambiguous, are incompatible. Effective

teams are able to clarify roles and manage any role conflicts that arise.

C. Interpersonal Issues (How are we going to get along?)
Many references are made, particularly in poorly functioning teams, to "personality clashes," "bad chemistry," and the like. The negative consequences of poor feelings between team members are not hard to recognize. The extent to which people trust, support, respect, and feel comfortable with one another can influence the effectiveness of teamwork.

D. Synergy Issues (How can we best learn from each other?)
One of the characteristics of a well-functioning team is that the team members take on the responsibility of "bringing everyone up to speed." A well-functioning team is like a hologram: The team's intelligence can be re-constructed from any team member. When operating effectively, teams are learning organizations.

E. Sanction Issues (What will we do with the deviate?)
How will the team deal with members who violate the agreed-upon norms of the team? Teams must develop ways of effectively dealing with the deviate, including the loafer. The sanctions must be clear and uniformly applied.

Finally: A Name and a Logo

After your team has prepared the first two sections of the team charter, create a name for your team and design a logo. The name and logo should be meaningful to the team, reflecting an attribute that the team members believe is important. The name is limited to one or two words. Write a brief explanation of your name and logo choice.

6

Managing Conflict

Using Reflective Listening to Manage Conflict

Students working together in a team may very well encounter some conflicts; that is not unusual. As the instructor, however, you cannot become the mediator and solve each team's problems. To manage conflict, you must help students create a constructive emotional climate when they are in a conflict situation. Some issues that may provoke tension include problems with unfair distribution of work, uneven quality of group work, poor attendance from a team member, or finding a satisfactory time to meet. If the students developed team charters, they may refer back to them for guidance. If not, the process begins by having students practice precise communication, using reflective listening to ensure mutual understanding. Creating a positive emotional environment through reflective listening is the first step in moving forward and resolving any differences that may exist within a team.

According to Syracuse University's Program on the Analysis and Resolution of Conflicts (PARC), managing conflict first begins with a level of awareness.

- The conflict must be recognized:
  "Uh, oh ... I feel anxious about ..."

- It must be named to other people within the group:
  "There's a problem with ..."

- Then the group must agree to work with the issue:
  "Are you willing to ..."

Once the group has agreed to work with the issue, the four basic steps of reflective listening can be adapted to managing the conflict. Reflective listening differs from typical listening in one significant way. Both types of listening involve gathering data, processing the data, and forming an hypothesis about what the other person has said. But the reflective listener in a fourth step then checks out the hypothesis with the speaker. Additionally, the reflective listener should be sensitive to cultural differences that impact communication. The listener should also pay close attention to the speaker's cues:

- visual (gestures, body language, facial expression)
- vocal (tone of voice, rate of speech, volume, inflections)
- verbal (content, key words or phrases, feeling words)
- contextual (where the communication is taking place)

Reflective Listening Exercise

This exercise gives students practice in listening reflectively and checking the hypothesis with the speaker. The observer practices giving feedback to the listener.

Use groups of three to four people. Each person selects a class-related topic or issue about which he or she feels strongly.

- X is the speaker who presents the topic or issue.
- Y practices the skills of reflective listening by taking in all the cues, processing and sorting them, and then reaching an hypothesis or a conclusion. (X is feeling _____ about _____.)
  Y then tests or checks the hypothesis with the speaker: You are _____(feeling word) about _____(content).
- Z watches for and records positive examples of the reflective listening skills that Y uses.

Example
After X finishes speaking, Y may hypothesize that X is feeling upset because John didn't do the research assignment that he was supposed to do for today's team meeting.

Y would then test or check the hypothesis with X by saying "You are feeling upset because John was supposed to do the research assignment for our meeting today, and he did not get it done."

Z would watch for and record positive examples of the reflective listening skills that Y uses. "You made good eye contact, you listened attentively, and the tone of your voice was helpful."

Role Rotation for Practicing Reflective Listening

Minutes 2–3	X Presents the topic or issue	Z Presents the topic or issue	Y Presents the topic or issue
2–3	Y Listens reflectively/ forms hypothesis and summarizes	X Listens reflectively/ forms hypothesis and summarizes	Z Listens reflectively/ forms hypothesis and summarizes
4	Z Watches for and records positive examples of the reflective listening skills that Y uses	Y Watches for and records positive examples of the reflective listening skills that X uses	X Watches for and records positive examples of the reflective listening skills that Z uses

Self-Analysis Format

This self-analysis exercise may be used immediately after the reflective listening exercise.

Answer the following questions concerning your behavior and feelings during the trio exercise just completed. Use a scale of 1 to 10, where 1 equals practically never and 10 equals almost always.

Practically Never	*Seldom*	*Sometimes*	*Usually*	*Almost Always*
1	3	5	7	10

Questions

Listening

1. Did I allow speakers to complete their thoughts or opinions without interrupting?   _____

2. Did I actively try to remember the important facts or points made by others?   _____

3. Did I jot down any details or points raised
   by others?   _____

4. Did I ever repeat back the gist of or summarize
   the points of view expressed by others?   _____

5. Did I keep an open mind even if I found the points
   made by others disagreeable?   _____

6. Did I avoid being hostile toward views that
   differed from my own?   _____

7. Did I express genuine interest in the
   conversation of others?   _____

Check the wording of each question carefully since the questions were phrased to suggest that a low number probably needs improvement.

Circle or jot down any area that you think needs improvement.

Dealing with Cultural Differences

When students work in teams, cultural issues may begin to influence the group's cohesiveness. Disparate ways of working in teams stem from different backgrounds and may be particularly significant with American students working with international students. However, if students are prepared to deal with these issues rather than avoiding them, they may understand each other's differences and learn to make accommodations. Students may also find that cultural differences can be described as stylistic differences, different ways of approaching tasks. As they work on tasks together, they should become aware of and sensitive to these differences.

Students should learn to acknowledge that different cultures have differing approaches to handling conflict. Americans traditionally want to confront the problem, but not all cultures find this acceptable. Reflective listening can be used to diffuse negative emotions that have arisen within a group. Each individual can have his or her position heard, and then the group works out the differences. But remember that reflective listening itself is a contemporary American practice; not everyone will feel comfortable with this approach.

According to Thomas and Kilmann (1974), all reactions that people have to conflict stem from two general responses. They have a desire to satisfy personal concerns, and this desire is demonstrated as assertive behavior, or they have a desire to satisfy the concerns of other people on the team, so they sublimate their concerns and demonstrate nonassertive behavior. Thomas and Kilmann describe these two kinds of behavior as conflict-handling modes.

General Suggestions for Teams

- Be thoughtful and sensitive to others.

- Respect each person as an individual.

- Recognize that we all may have absorbed some biases about other cultures.

- Avoid "distributing" minority students so that a class of 30 students, 25 whites and five African Americans or five Asian women, has five groups with one minority student in each group. This "equitable" distribution according to Rosser (1998) may be harmful to the minority students.

- When the teams form, have each team member take time to share things that make him or her feel comfortable or uncomfortable about working in teams.

- Encourage a three-second rule between speakers because other cultures may need room to speak and find it culturally impolite to interrupt. If a group member has something to say immediately after someone has spoken, it may mean the person was planning what to say and was not listening very carefully to the speaker.

- Expect the same level of quality work from all group members.

- Try to make the team's project inclusive; i.e., including information or research related to typically underrepresented groups, classes, races, or genders. This information should be integrated into the topic, not making it a special topic or appendix.

Long-Term Maintenance of Teams

The difficulties that teams face when doing a project over a short period of time may become accentuated when teams have a long-term project to complete. First, review the section on establishing a climate for supporting teams (Chapter 1). A good climate and a clear structure at the beginning will ease the maintenance process. Remember that team members doing long-term projects also go through the same team social dynamics that were described in Part I of this book: forming, storming, norming, and performing.

When a team is in Stage One (Forming), the anxiety levels are high for both short-term and long-term projects. It is especially important that a team that will be working together for a lengthy project get off to a good start because more is at stake for both the students and the instructor. The guidelines for student teams (Chapter 4) give suggestions for clarifying team communication at the very beginning, for example, setting up team member roles and discussing the decisions teams must make about how their team meetings will function. Any of the team exercises that are described in Chapter 5 can be used to acquaint the team members with each other and to develop team spirit. Requiring the teams to do the team charter assignment (Chapter 5) forces them to develop ground rules for attendance, lateness, interruptions, decision-making, and other issues that the team will face over time. Doing everything that you can to have the teams establish clear ground rules and good communication at the beginning of a project can prevent many problems.

Inevitably, Stage Two (Storming) develops as teams encounter some areas of disagreement. This is a good time to have students refer back to their team charters, review their ground rules, and make sure their procedures are working. You can also use the material on resolving conflicts and the reflective listening exercise (this chapter) at this stage. You may also want to review the material presented earlier in this chapter on dealing with cultural differences or have students do an exercise on preferred learning styles such as "How Do I Learn Best?" (Chapter 3). Team members may also use the team member reaction form (Chapter 7) for analyzing how their team is functioning and determining what the problems are. Sometimes it is necessary for the instructor to meet with teams that are having difficulty to help them verbalize their issues and concerns.

Teams finally reach Stage Three (Norming) when their members understand exactly what they have to do to complete their project by the deadline. At this point the students are more independent, and they do not have as many questions. One helpful item that can be used now is the team meeting self-analysis form (Chapter 4); it helps students assess and reflect on their role during team meetings. Students also continue to use the team meeting report (Chapter 4) to report on their meetings and to keep track of decisions and future agendas. Now is the time to begin focusing on evaluation and how the team members can respond with constructive criticism to the work produced by other members of their team. Students should be focusing on the final product and trying to make sure that each member contributes as equally as possible to the final product.

During Stage Four (Performing), members are completing their team project and working well as a team as they support each other's efforts. Teams should be given an opportunity to reflect on their accomplishments and what they have learned from working as a team. Students should also fill out the team member peer evaluation form in Chapter 7.

References

McKenna, S. (1995). The business impact of management attitudes towards dealing with conflict: A cross-cultural assessment. *Journal of Managerial Psychology, 10* (7).

Rosser, S. (1998, Summer). Group work in science, engineering, and mathematics: Consequences of ignoring gender and race. *College Teaching, 64* (3), 82–88.

Thomas, K. W., & Kilmann, R. H. (1974). *The Thomas-Kilmann conflict mode instrument.* Tuxedo, NY: Xicom.

7

Team Evaluation

Team Member Reaction

This form helps students analyze how their team is working and also assists the instructor in checking how the teams are functioning.

Circle the response that best reflects your feelings.

1. To what extent do you actually participate in the team?

    a. Not at all

    b. Very little

    c. Quite a lot

    d. Very much

2. How well does the group work at its task?

    a. Works very hard, is achieving its goal

    b. Works well, is making definite progress

    c. Has made some progress, some members loaf

    d. Has made no progress at all

3. To what extent has the group talked about its own functioning as a team, and to what extent does the group talk about other topics?

    a. Almost completely on outside problems or topics

    b. More about outside topics than ourselves

    c. More about ourselves than outside topics

    d. Almost completely on ourselves and our own group

4. To what extent have members been out to win their own points as opposed to considering the merits of the issues?

    a. Almost completely out to win their own points

    b. Occasionally out to win their own points

    c. Seldom out to win their own points

    d. Almost completely considered merits of the issues

5. To what extent have you had thoughts and unexpressed feelings and opinions that you have not felt comfortable bringing out in the team?

    a. I felt completely free and expressive

    b. I felt somewhat free and expressive

    c. I felt somewhat under wraps

    d. I felt completely under wraps

6. To what extent have minority views been listened to with respect?

    a. Most are disregarded or ignored

    b. A lot are ignored

    c. A lot are listened to

    d. Most are given thought and consideration

7. What does the team generally do when confronted with differences in feelings and ideas?

    a. Avoid discussion of apparent differences

    b. Recognize differences but move quickly on to other topics

    c. Faces conflict but does not manage it well

    d. Faces conflicts openly and works them through

8. To what extent do you feel a real part of the team?

    a. Completely a part of the team

    b. Mostly a part of the team

    c. Mostly on the outside of the team

    d. Completely on the outside, not part of the team at all

9. At the moment, to what extent do you believe you could work effectively with this team in the future?

   a. Not at all

   b. Not very much

   c. Quite a lot

   d. A great deal

Team Member Peer Evaluation

Have students use this form for evaluating their peers when completing a team project. It gives students an opportunity to give feedback on individual efforts during a project. Instructors will find this form useful for determining individual effort on projects.

Team Name/Number: _____

In the space provided below, please list the names of your team members—including yourself—and circle the number that *best* describes each team member's contribution to the team project, using the following scale. You may also comment on each team member's contribution.

10 **Full participation.** This individual was a true team player; he or she made significant content and process contributions throughout the semester and was clearly committed to making the whole project a success.

8 **Strong selective participation.** This individual made a significant contribution to the project, but within a clearly defined scope; he or she limited participation to a particular content or process role—and showed initiative in that area—but did not view the overall project as his or her responsibility.

6 **Selective participation.** This individual made a contribution to the project, but the contribution was rather narrow; her or his work was of good quality, but of minimum quantity.

4 Weak participation. This individual attended project meetings but made little substantive contribution to the content or the process of the project; he or she showed little initiative and contributed only what was specifically requested.

2 Virtually absent. This individual frequently missed project meetings, often came unprepared, or contributed substandard work that required correction by fellow team members; he or she exhibited very little effort and made minimal contribution to the project.

0 Totally absent. This individual was totally absent from the project, and the end product in no way reflects a contribution on her or his part.

Name	Score	Comments
1.	0 2 4 6 8 10	
2.	0 2 4 6 8 10	
3.	0 2 4 6 8 10	
4.	0 2 4 6 8 10	
5.	0 2 4 6 8 10	
6.	0 2 4 6 8 10	
7.	0 2 4 6 8 10	

Use the back of this form for additional comments as needed.

Final Evaluation of Individual Contributions to the Team Project

Here is another sample form for evaluating individual contributions to a team project. This form may also be used if there are intermediate assignments during the semester. Early feedback is important for changing behavior.

Team Number _____

Team Member Evaluated: _____

A. Rank this individual on the following attributes
   (mark appropriate box):

Attribute	Excellent 5	Good 4	Average 3	Fair 2	Poor 1	None 0
Attendance at team meetings						
Quality of participation in discussions						
Quantity of participation in discussions						
Ability to focus on purpose of meetings						
Attitude toward team						
Attitude toward team project						
Promptness in meeting team deadlines						
Leadership skills						
Followership skills						
Team-building skills						
Listening skills						
Quality of research contribution						
Quantity of research contribution						
Quality of writing contribution						
Quantity of writing contribution						
Quality of editing contribution						
Quantity of editing contribution						
Overall evaluation of contribution to team project						

B. Provide a narrative evaluation of this individual's performance to
   support the rankings you made above. Give specific examples to support your rankings.

Team Meeting Self-Analysis

Encourage students to use this form to monitor their own behavior in team meetings over time.

Date _____

Answer the following questions concerning your behavior during the team meeting just completed. Use a scale of 1 to 10 where *1 = Practically Never* and *10 = Almost Always*:

Practically Never	Seldom	Sometimes	Usually	Almost Always
1	3	5	7	10

Question	Score	Improve?
1. Did I allow speakers to complete their thoughts or opinions without interrupting?		
2. Did I actively try to remember the important facts or points made by others?		
3. Did I jot down any details or points raised by others?		
4. Did I ever repeat back the gist of or summarize the points of view expressed by others?		
5. Did I keep an open mind even if I found the points made by others disagreeable?		
6. Did I avoid being hostile toward the views that differed from my own?		
7. Did I express genuine interest in the conversation of others?		

Once you have scored your behavior by answering each of the above questions, indicate in the last column any behaviors that you think might need improvement.

This form is a useful tool for you to use to monitor your behavior in team meetings over time. Please fill it out at the end of each team meeting. It is for your own evaluation and use; it will not be turned in.

Team Meeting Report

Teams should use this sheet for reporting on their meetings and for keeping track of decisions and future agendas. Copies of reports may be given to each team member and to the instructor.

Team Meeting Report

Date

Present:

Absent:

What Happened:

Decisions/Action Items: Person Responsible:

By when?

Agenda for next meeting: Date, time, and place:

Coordinator for next meeting: _____

Timekeeper/recorder for next meeting: _____

This team meeting report is my interpretation of what happened at this meeting. Let me know if there are any errors.

Recorder _____

Top-Notch Tips for Team Learning

Introductory Discussion

Twenty-three University of Minnesota, Duluth faculty members met bimonthly during the 1995–1996 year to learn more about and to share their experiences in using cooperative learning in the classroom. Funded by the Bush Foundation through a grant received by the Instructional Development Service, they are members of the Bush Interdisciplinary Group for Faculty Development. Their focus is cooperative learning.

Even though cooperative learning has a rather specific definition and techniques, this group chose to include both in-class and out-of-class cooperative strategies as well as collaborative methods as fair game for investigation. In fact, to avoid terminology that might confine or constrict the experiments, the group sanctioned calling its focus team learning.

In keeping with the team spirit, then, the Bush Group/Team offers these tips to faculty who want to incorporate more cooperative learning into their teaching. Although this list of tips is not meant to be comprehensive, nor even original, it is meant to be pragmatic.

On Your Mark

- The bottom line: Play to your strengths. Collaborative teaching is not for everyone nor appropriate for every occasion. But if you use it, always have a printed time for the exercise. If I think it should take 30 minutes, I put down 20. I can always lengthen it if it appears that everyone is on track. Too long and the students become restless. If I notice that 50% of the students are done early, I close the exercise. So far no one has noticed that I can't tell time.

  Linda Parry, Management Studies

- At an IDS workshop I heard a suggestion about educating our students about the value of cooperative/collaborative learning before using it in the classroom because it is usually so new to them. I have a mini-lecture from that workshop that I use in courses where a lot of such group work will be used in class. It's a bit "cheesy," but it gets the point across on cooperative versus competitive. This preteaching, though time-consuming at the beginning, seems to help. In addition, if students are unfamiliar with cooperative or group learning, it can also be helpful to teach them a bit about how to work effectively in groups.

    Paula Pedersen-Randall, Psychology

- During the first session of the tutor training class, I ask students to form groups of three or four to discuss what concerns them about their new endeavor. When the groups report back to the whole class, students find that their classmates' anxieties mirror their own. During this report-back session, we also discuss the resources we have for overcoming whatever potential problems they have cited. At the same time I insert information about the course syllabus that pertains to class sessions that treat these concerns—a much nicer way to cover the syllabus without spending the entire first session lecturing. I think this would be equally effective in any class with high-anxiety material.

    Jill Strand, Achievement Center and UC

- Discuss the various interdependent roles that members assume in a cooperative learning group. For example, *functional roles* may include recorder, spokesperson, social-process monitor; *perspective roles* may include ethical, economic, cultural, global...; *cognitive roles* might be analysis, synthesis, evaluation, elaboration, application....

    Pat Hamon, UC/University for Seniors

- When using cooperative learning groups in large classes, a major problem is make-up work. Don't try to evaluate people's reasons for missing a class or meeting. Allow students to make up any group assignment, but be sure that the make-up assignment is 1) somewhat harder than the group session, and 2) something that really enhances your course objectives. For example, to make up one of the 15 group assignments in my Sociology and Social Problems course, students must attend a lecture on campus (from an approved list that I post outside the classroom) and write a two- to three-page paper according to guidelines I provide.

Bruce Mork, Sociology/Anthropology

Get Ready

- When assigning the task, make sure that everyone understands the vocabulary in the directions and that everyone knows what you are talking about. Keep the jargon to a minimum. For example, in a session about doing a computer search, if I were to ask a group of students to construct a search using Boolean logic, they would need to know what Boolean means.

  Pam Enrici, Library

- Those who have students involved in cooperative or collaborative learning in their classes find that the amount of time the instructor spends working with groups to explain assignment details, expectations, and grading after making an assignment is inversely related to the amount of time spent developing them and the specificity of the directions given to groups before they start working on the assignment. Thus, to maximize the relatively limited time the instructor has available to observe or do things other than talk about assignment details and requirements after groups begin to work, the instructor should provide clear and understandable directions and answer as many questions as possible before groups begin their work.

  Tom Duff, FMIS

- The best way I have found to ensure that students follow the directions is:

  1) To provide written directions—on the board/overhead/poster paper, or if lengthy, on paper with one set per group. If there is only one set, the students then tend to work more as a group. If they all get a copy, they read on their own, and it tends to fragment the operation.

  2) To explain the task orally, pointing to the written steps on the board.

3) If the task is complicated, to model it (mini role play) with some students so everyone can see how things work.
Helen Rallis, Education

- I believe that groups need to establish a comfort (trust) level in order to function well, so I try to make sure that there is time during group work for students to get to know each other and bond a bit. Simple icebreakers can help with this. Names, hobbies, interests, and aspirations are all things students can share to get to know each other. Also, some simple values clarification exercises can be helpful. All of this aids the maintenance function in the group.
Dale S. Olson, Achievement Center

- Initial team building activities help create a sense of group identity and cohesion. I would suggest hands-on experiences such as building towers with spaghetti and marshmallows, building bridges with newspapers and masking tape, or creating a sculpture with a variety of recyclables. They are good ice breakers, involve a variety of learning styles, and make tangible the need for each member to be involved for the group project to be successful.
Pat Hamon, UC/University for Seniors

- Before using small groups in class to work on case studies, I first work through at least one or two similar cases on an overhead. This modeling leads to a greater sense of success in small groups.
LaVonne Levar, Communication Sciences & Disorders

- Consistently now I have "repeat clientele"—students I see more than twice in teacher preparation classes. This quarter I have begun to use cooperative methods which pair the class members in two ways: 1) mentor and rookie, or 2) teaching partners. The first pairing is made on the basis of having the same off-campus school placement. The mentor can answer many questions for the rookie more quickly than I can because of just having worked on the site. If there is a problem, it lies in the mentors not knowing just how much they should do.
Donna Misslitz, Health, Physical Education and Recreation

Get Set

- An intervention is a thoughtful way or means for achieving a result. Simple tables, grids, or charts act as good interventions in abetting cooperative interaction in the classroom. Giving students a visual framework to fill in as they record the results of their group activities assists them in staying on task.

  Kathleen Nuccio, Social Work

- In collaboratively creating their own textbook, my students commented on how effective the jigsaw approach was in fostering responsibility to the group. The students found the jigsaws to be a great learning experience and that participating in them really tightened up those sections of their papers which were jigsawed.

  Sheryl Grana, Sociology/Anthropology

- The jigsaw approach works well with theories in psychology classes.

  Paula Pedersen-Randall, Psychology

- For group learning in class, I often use the "think-pair-share" method intermixed with lectures. After covering a certain amount of material, I ask either a summarizing or an application question and tell the class to first think about the question, then pair with a classmate and share their thoughts. Finally, the whole class hears from several pairs on how they answered the given question. This method helps students summarize what's been covered so far, and it definitely breaks the monotony of lectures.

  Aydin Durgunoglu, Psychology

- This is the first quarter I have used folders to expedite group work. They are great! For a class of 40, I put together nine or ten folders (depending on the exercise) and include all the materials needed for the exercise. The groups return the folders at the end of the period. Using folders is a neat, clean way of facilitating the process. It also forces me to think ahead of exactly everything that everyone will need and allows me to use collaborative exercises in classes of 40, something that would have been difficult previously.

  Linda Parry, Management Studies

- There is a great deal of value in going around and monitoring groups as they work. It helps to keep them on task, and it helps you to see if they really know what it is that you want them to be doing. In addition, the instructor can provide valuable input from one group to another that helps to further the process. If the group work is being done outside of class, it is also important to have a paper version of a process check.

Diane Rauschenfels, Education

- When my collaborative writing groups are in the planning stages (particularly for their first meeting), they get more done if I ask them to turn in minutes of their meeting. This forces them to stick to the task at hand and to make decisions as to the schedule, who is going to do what, etc. It also gives them a record of those decisions (I am always amazed at how many don't write down any of this information if they aren't asked to). Interestingly, I find that I often have to explain what minutes are. They aren't used to attending meetings where minutes are taken and aren't always familiar with what they should include.

Jill Jenson, Composition

- Approximately three times during the quarter, I ask for written feedback from the groups on their projects. Using one of Angelo and Cross' Classroom Assessment Techniques, I ask each group to provide me with information on how many times the group met, how many members are in the group, how many participate actively most of the time, how effectively the group is working together (from poorly to very well), and, most important, what one change the group could make to improve its performance.

Cindy Spillers, Communication Sciences and Disorders

The Finish Line

- I have successfully used the paired annotations format described by Barbara Millis in her article, "Increasing Thinking through Cooperative Writing." (To create student pairs, I use a deck of cards.) The value is in the intensity of the dialogue created by pairs compared to that of a whole group discussing content. When students do the same exercises and then review them as pairs, a great deal of learning occurs. As they finish their paired discussions, I ask each pair to write one critical point or statement on the white/ black board. This allows for whole group interaction and an opportunity to see if there are recurrent themes across pairs.

Noell Reinhiller, Education

- I try to structure tasks for small groups in such a way that group results can be put on the board by a group member. For example, when studying mnemonic devices in my study strategies class recently, I asked each group to create a mnemonic from a list of memory principles. Then each group put its mnemonic on the board and explained it to the whole class. We then discussed the results and the limitations of mnemonics. This is helpful because 1) each group is accountable for a product that will be shared with the class (this increases the likelihood that groups will stay on task and feel an investment in their results), and 2) it gives me a chance to look over the results and think about my responses. No matter how much time I devote to anticipating possibilities, I am frequently caught off guard by a group's response. Comfort levels are important to instructors as well as students.

Kathleen Clark, Achievement Center

- Since I often have not been satisfied with the work that students complete in small group work, I have decided to go around to each group to go over the marked and graded work I have returned to them, rather than just leave it up to them to look over the returned papers.

Tom Farrell, Composition

- Videotaping students' presentations and placing the tapes on reserve in the library has several advantages. If students miss class, they need not miss seeing other group products. Furthermore, students can view their own performances and begin to internalize their own standards for evaluation.

Tom Duff, FMIS

- When assigning group work, include an example of how you are going to grade. If you can include some humor in it, all the better. For example, on a recent multimedia project which accounted for ten percent of the overall grade, I showed my class that I would evaluate each group's project on a 30-point scale based on five criteria, then multiply those points by the number of students in the group, e.g., a group of five earning 25 points on their project would amass 125 points. The group then would decide among themselves how to allocate those 125 points to the individual members of the group. For instance:

Energetic Ellen	35 pts
Dozing Donna	15 pts
Absent Al	5 pts
Creative Carl	35 pts
Cooperative Charlie	35 pts

  The statistician for the group would report the allocation of the points to the instructor.

  Alan Roline, Business Law

- Make work available for others to see. This results in students putting more energy, effort, time, and pride into their work. While there are many ways to display work, I recently learned that there is a simple means for students to post their work on homepages (without being personally identified) so that other students or interested people can react to it.

  Pat Hamon, UC/University for Seniors

Three specific cooperative learning techniques were mentioned in this chapter: jigsaw, think-pair-share, and paired annotations. If you are interested in the mechanics of these techniques, they are described in *Active Learning: Co-Operation in the College Classroom* by Johnson, Johnson, and Smith.

"Here's one that has worked for me: Top-notch tips for team learning" was originally printed in Rutherford, L. H. (Ed.). (1996). Instructional development, xii (3). Duluth, MN: University of Minnesota, Duluth. Reprinted with permission.

References

Millis, B. (1994, Spring). Increasing thinking through cooperative writing. *Cooperative Learning and College Teaching, 4* (3), 7-8.

Johnson, D. W., Johnson, R. T., & Smith, K. A. (1998). *Active learning: Co-Operation in the college classroom* (2nd ed.). Edina, MN: Interaction Book Co.

III

PART

Teamwork
in the Disciplines

Architecture
Behavioral Ecology
Introductory Ceramics
Child and Family Studies
Distance Learning, Technology, and Teamwork
Education
Engineering
English and Textual Studies
Fine Arts
Health and Exercise Science
Higher Education
Management
Mathematics
Nursing
Nutrition and the Hospitality and Food Service
Management Programs
Public Affairs
Sociology
Writing

Architecture:
Team Competitions

Ivan Markov
School of Architecture, Syracuse University

Introductory Discussion

The Bridge Project that is described here is part of a course on architectural structures. The project gives architecture students an opportunity to work in teams and to practice the structural theory that they have been learning. The major benefit of the team project is that the students are both teachers and learners at the same time. They have to discuss the issues, and they practice working as a team. The disadvantage is that sometimes the projects may take too much of the students' time and too much presentation time.

For the Bridge Project, each team of students works together to design and construct a bridge model; then the students test the bridge for how much weight it can hold. The students have to predict the exact location where the bridge will fail and the load that will cause the bridge to fail. Each team presents its bridge project in class and actually tests the bridge.

Another team project in the course involves a model competition. The students are divided into teams and are expected to build a model that is judged in a class competition. Generally, three teams are assigned to each type of model, and the teams present their projects to the entire class. The students act as jurors and grade the teams.

Activity 1: Bridge Project

Students are given the following problem: Design, analyze, construct, and test a bridge model. The only criterion is the efficiency of the bridge. The efficiency is defined as the ratio between failure load and the bridge weight. Students must comply with the following.

- *Loading.* Loading will be applied at the deck through the loading block at the mid span. You are responsible for leaving sufficient room for the loading block. Load failure is defined on another sheet (not included here).

- *Testing.* On the day of testing, each team is required to present its project. The presentation has to be two minutes long. Team members should be as professional as possible and include the most important information. During the presentation, teams are required to predict the location of the failure and the ultimate load. A one-minute discussion may follow the test. Participation of all students in the discussion is strongly encouraged. The testing may be videotaped.

Instructions for the Instructor
The instructors must obtain or assemble the kits for the projects and set up the schedule for the project and presentations.

Set-Up and Materials
Students work in teams of six; they pick their own teams because they know each others' schedules. They need to arrange time to work together with their team that is not part of the studio time.

Each team receives a kit, and the bridge must be constructed only from the material that is in the kit: structural members of balsa wood, precut balsa wood gusset plates for connections, and glue. They may not use any other glue. They may use computer programs for preliminary structural analyses. The testing lab will provide a loading block.

Time Frame/Schedule
Students work on these projects outside of class. They generally have several weeks to do the project. On average, students each spend 10–15 hours on the project.

Follow-Up and/or Assessment
Team grades are based on the following: efficiency (50%), creativity (30%), and presentation with discussion and failure prediction (20%).

Activity 2: Model Competition

Students are again divided into teams for this competition. The teams build four different kinds of models that are then demonstrated in class; each team is evaluated by the other teams that do not have the same model topic. The types of models that students can build include the following:

- Build a model to demonstrate the effect of cross-sectional shape, support conditions and connections on strength, stiffness, and stability of structure subject to gravity loads. (Hint: roller, pin, fixed, continuous, hinge, rigid, moment of inertia, etc.)

- Build a model to demonstrate the external and internal stability of structure subject to lateral loads. (Hint: overturning, sliding, bracing, shear walls, connections, etc.)

- Build a model to demonstrate the presence of internal forces such as axial, shear, and moments in structure. (Hint: elements, load, span, equilibrium, etc.)

- Build a model to demonstrate the effect of axial load (tension and compression on structural members). (Hint: buckling, length, support conditions, cross-section, direction of buckling, crushing, cables, etc.)

Notes

- *Requirements:* Models must be reusable and should not exceed the size of 3'x3'x1'

- *Materials:* ANY (Hint: wood, cardboard, paper, Styrofoam, glue, sponge, plasticine, etc.)

- *Equipment:* ANY (Hint: scale, weights, boxes, tape measure, string, spring scale, tape, ruler, etc.)

- *Scale:* Sufficient to serve the purpose

- *Presentation:* Maximum time (8 minutes)

- *Cost:* Approximately $60 per group

- *Ownership:* The school will keep the models

Time Frame/Schedule

Students work on these projects outside of class. They generally have several weeks to do the project.

Follow Up and/or Assessment

Models are graded on the following criteria: effectiveness (50%), creativity (30%), presentation (20%).

After students present their models in class, the students use an evaluation form similar to the one on the next page to evaluate each model. Students are not permitted to evaluate groups that are within their model topic.

Sample rating sheet that can be used for the competition.

Model Competition

Group_____ Name _____

Average time spent per person: _____

Grading: A, A–, B+, B, B–, C+, C, C–, D, F

Note: Do not grade groups within your topic.

Section Shape	Effectiveness	Creativity	Presentation
1 _____	_____	_____	_____
2 _____	_____	_____	_____
3 _____	_____	_____	_____

Overall Stability	Effectiveness	Creativity	Presentation
4 _____	_____	_____	_____
5 _____	_____	_____	_____
6 _____	_____	_____	_____

Internal Forces	Effectiveness	Creativity	Presentation
7 _____	_____	_____	_____
8 _____	_____	_____	_____
9 _____	_____	_____	_____

Columns	Effectiveness	Creativity	Presentation
10 _____	_____	_____	_____
11 _____	_____	_____	_____
12 _____	_____	_____	_____

Bridge	Effectiveness	Creativity	Presentation
13 _____	_____	_____	_____
14 _____	_____	_____	_____
15 _____	_____	_____	_____

Behavioral Ecology: Team Activities in the Field

Larry L. Wolf
Biology Department, Syracuse University

Introductory Discussion

The two projects that are described in this section are taught as part of a field course at the Cranberry Lake Biological Station in the Adirondacks. The course, Behavioral Ecology, is a two-week course that is taught to juniors and seniors enrolled at the State University of New York College of Environmental Science & Forestry. The course introduces students to the process of doing field work in behavioral ecology. Several team projects are used to teach students how to gather, analyze, and interpret field data.

To get enough information in a one-day project, group projects are a necessity. The students use teams for collecting data; the team size depends upon the project.

Activity 1: Bumblebees

Do bumblebees have rules for how they move between consecutive flowers? For this activity, students study whether bumblebees have rules when feeding on flowers. As they move around the landscape, are they clever enough to stay in areas where there is lots of nectar and move out of areas where there is no nectar? If they do stay in areas where there is lots of nectar, how do they do it?

Instructions for the Instructor

- Have a supply of "flags" for the students to use.
- Students need a data book.

Set-Up and Materials

Students are put into teams of five, and each student has a job. One student has to track the bee. A second student records the data; e.g., how long does the bee remain at each flower? The other three students flag each flower so that they can trace the route of the bee over 20 or 30 flowers where the bee has stopped. When they finish collecting the data, the students then map the path of the bee. When the group starts to collect data on additional bees, they switch roles to give each student an opportunity to practice different tasks.

Time Frame/Schedule

Students spend one day on this activity. During the data collecting, each group can usually study two or three bees. After they collect the data, they spend some time in the afternoon analyzing what they have collected and interpreting the results in the context of optimal foraging theory.

Follow-Up and/or Assessment

The purpose of this exercise is to learn the process of collecting, analyzing, and interpreting data in the field. The quality of the information that students collect may not be great. The real assessment comes when they do their own projects later in the course.

Activity 2: Damselfly Mating Behavior

What is the mating behavior of male damselflies? In advance of the students' arrival at the field site, the males are marked. The students work in teams of two. Each team finds and follows a single male damselfly. One student watches what the fly is doing and informs his or her partner, who is the recorder, of the fly's actions. The recorder's job is to keep track of the observations. Halfway through the exercise, the students switch roles. After the individual teams have collected their data, they go back to the lab and work as a large group of eight to 16 students to analyze the data to describe the mating system of this population.

Instructions for the Instructor

- The male damselflies must be marked before the students begin the activity.

- Students need a data book.

Set-Up and Materials

Students work in pairs, and each student has a job. One student is the observer and has to tell his or her partner what the fly is doing. The second student works as the recorder and writes down what the first student has observed. Halfway through the exercise, the students reverse roles to give both students the opportunity to observe and to record.

Time Frame/Schedule

Students spend one day on this activity. During this time, they may study two or three damselflies. After the individual groups have collected their data, they go back to the lab and work as a large group of eight to 16 students to analyze the data.

Follow-Up and/or Assessment

The purpose of this exercise is to learn the process and to describe the mating system of the damselfly. The quality of the information that the students collect may not be great. The real assessment comes when they do their own projects later in the course.

Introductory Ceramics: Collaborative Art Projects

Errol Willet
School of Visual and Performing Arts,
Syracuse University

Introductory Discussion

In my introductory handbuilding course in ceramics, the use of collaborative projects is helpful in many ways. It loosens the students up and eliminates some of the inhibitions many people experience when working with new and unfamiliar materials. It allows students to see a variety of solutions they might not have imagined. It challenges standard notions of ownership and provides students with a design team model similar to many professional art-commission situations.

Activity 1: The Collaborative Teapot

Teapots are made up of several parts: the body, spout, lid, and handle. Each student is asked to make three spouts, three handles, three lids, and three bodies (or pots), and to bring them to the next class in the "leather hard" stage of dryness (this is a stage when the clay is holding its shape and is no longer sticky or soft but is still capable of being cut and joined together). All the parts are spread across a table, and the students draw numbers from a hat to pick parts. The only rule is that they cannot pick the parts they made themselves. From these randomly chosen parts, they assemble teapots. What was a spout for the maker becomes a lid or handle for the builder. What was right-side-up in one person's eye is turned upside down and cut in half to another. This tends to challenge one's perception of forms. When the teapots are assembled, I ask everyone to pass their teapot to the person next to them for painting. Now a new person is asked to apply color to the forms someone else assembled from parts made by others. The removal of ownership or responsibility for prior decisions in the artwork seems to give each participant in the teapot activity more freedom to take risks.

Instructions for the Instructor

- You will need some clay, slips, and glaze that are compatible. It doesn't have to be too complicated for success. A red clay with black and white slips and a clear glaze work well.

- This project works best toward the end of the semester after some basic instruction in the possibilities and methods of these forms.

- Stress to the students that the forms they select from the table do not have to be used "as is" in their teapot, but can be altered in any way to meet their vision.

Time Frame/Schedule

One week to make parts. One class (at least three hours) to construct teapots. One class to paint or decorate (one to three hours). Use part of an additional class to look at finished pieces from kiln and discuss.

Assessment/Group Discussion of Finished Work

Allow students to find the parts they made within the teapots someone else constructed and talk about how they were used in ways they didn't expect. Within the broadest parameters defining teapots—i.e., spout extending higher than lid, ability to hold liquid, handle you can grasp in some way, spout that pours—talk about forms and ideas that are surprising, that push the boundaries, and are unusual juxtapositions of forms.

Alternative Project Ideas

Do the same project using parts of the human figure instead of teapots.

Introductory Discussion

With my intermediate and advanced ceramics students, I use a team project to build a large-scale sculpture. This project reinforces concepts of design and the necessity for preliminary sketches and models. It also shows the students the importance of a group effort in making artwork of a scale where many hours of labor are involved.

Activity 2: Architectural Ceramic Sculpture

One project we did recently was a tile-covered outdoor bench, approximately eight feet long. Each student in the class is assigned to draw designs for an outdoor bench on sketchbook paper. All designs are collected, critiqued as a group, and voted on. Three designs are chosen by a class vote, and all students are assigned to build three-dimensional models of one of the three chosen designs. Models at this stage should include color and tile design ideas.

Variations of the three chosen designs are acceptable at this stage as long as they relate clearly to one of the three drawings. Again, the group comes together and critiques the models and votes, this time selecting one winner. Once the final design is chosen, the class is divided into one team that fabricates the structure of the bench, a second group that builds the tile, and a third group that makes the glazes and decorates the tile. The student whose design is finally chosen takes on the role of project leader. This task involves overseeing all aspects of the project and is a great learning tool for teaching people skills, group decision-making dynamics, and group communication. All three groups share in the final tile setting and grouting. (Don't worry. I didn't know anything about tile when I started this. It wasn't hard and was extremely empowering to learn.)

Instructions for the Instructor

- You will need some clay, slips, and glaze that are compatible. It doesn't have to be too complicated for success. Stoneware and porcelain glazes will hold up better in harsh climates. Glaze colorants or mason stains can be used to color the grout to work with your glaze or clay. I buy white grout and color it in the studio.

- You will need something for the structure of the bench. If you can build it on site you can use heavier materials like concrete or stone. Otherwise, plywood or concrete board dur-rock work well. For the tiles, you will need tile adhesive and grout. Epoxy grout is extremely waterproof, but expensive and tricky to apply. Standard grout is fine. For large grout spaces which most handmade tiles require, a sanded grout is recommended.

- Tools: A shallow plastic tub for mixing mortar or grout. Trowels—at least one V-notched trowel for adhesive (an inexpensive plastic one works fine). A grouting trowel made of rubber or foam. Some foam core or cardboard and paints for models. Other materials may be required, depending upon the particular bench design. (Again, don't worry; you can do this.)

Time Frame/Schedule
At Syracuse University, one class equals five hours. This is only an estimate of the time needed for this project. One class for concept discussion, slide presentation of architectural tile work, and to begin drawings of bench designs. A second class for three-dimensional models. Two classes for construction of bench and tiles and glazes. Two classes for construction/tile-setting/installation.

Assessment/Group Discussion of Finished Work
Sit on and around your new bench, take a break, contemplate your surroundings, and talk about how the project evolved/mutated/changed through the various design and construction phases. Talk about the group dynamic, the various roles people assumed, how creative and process decisions were made, and how the bench looks and feels.

Alternative Project Ideas
Archways, walls, doorways, walkways.

Child and Family Studies: Team Service-Learning

Mellisa Clawson
Department of Child and Family Studies,
Syracuse University

Introductory Discussion

Language development is complex and varies with the age of the child. The students in a language development class were asked to apply their learning about language by developing a service project that would meet a language need in the community. Because books and reading help to develop language skills, the students chose a book drive as the service-learning project. With the help of the local Child Care Council, the class located three child care facilities in need of books. The students then researched the language development of the children in these locations, planned and implemented fundraising for the books, and organized literacy events at each of the locations. A useful reference for this project is Clawson and Couse's article, "Service Learning as a Teaching Strategy in Human Development and Family Studies Courses."

Activity: Service-Learning as a Teaching Strategy

The students divided the service-learning project into three phases: research, fundraising, and a literacy event. Ten to 12 students worked on each phase. In the research phase, students visited child care centers to observe the language development of the children and to determine the needs in each classroom. In the fundraising phase, donations were solicited from the campus and community. The response was overwhelming: More than 950 books were collected. Additionally, writing supplies, games, markers, paint, and Play-Doh were donated. Scholastic Incorporated made a donation of several dozen books.

In the final phase of the project, students organized literacy events at each of the centers. The students presented the books and materials to the classrooms and planned activities to help children develop a love of reading. Together the students and the children attending day care read many books, learned from each other, and shared a common language.

A different project is usually done each semester. The instructor contacts some community agencies to determine needs and wish lists and then communicates several options to the class; the students then decide which project(s) to pursue. In the language class that did the literacy project, the class as a whole completed one project. However, in larger classes (65 students or more), several service-learning projects are conducted simultaneously (e.g., a pancake breakfast to benefit a foundation for sickle cell anemia, a holiday party in the children's oncology ward at University Hospital). A few are described in the article mentioned above. In the larger classes, all students participated in all three phrases of the service-learning process.

Set-Up and Materials

The instructor has implemented service-learning in courses ranging from ten to 65 students. This literacy project was conducted in a class of approximately 40 students, so there were ten to14 students per phase. At the beginning of the semester, students are assigned to groups. The instructor sets up the groups to reflect the diversity of the class. Age, race, gender, experience, and academic major are taken into consideration. Because this project is a major component of the course, groups are provided with class time for meeting.

At Syracuse University, the Center for Public and Community Service helps faculty to set up service-learning projects. Other campuses may have their own centers that serve as excellent resources.

Time Frame/Schedule
Sample Schedule

Phase I: Research

January 20–27	Planning
February 3–10	Site visits
February 24	Oral reports to class

Phase II: Fundraising
        February 24–March 3   Planning
        March 3–17   Fundraising
        March 24   Oral report to class

Phase III: Event
        March 3–31   Planning
        April 7–14   "Literacy Event"
        April 21   Oral report to class

Follow-Up and/or Assessment

Each group is expected to do oral presentations to the class. After the research phase, students do the oral presentation to justify why their particular issue deals with a community need. For example, the group that decides to study language development in day care centers must visit the sites and assess the language needs at each site.

During the implementation phase, each group must prepare a written proposal for a service-learning project and then implement the project. The proposal must include a description of the project, a timeline, and how the project will be evaluated.

After the project is completed, students reflect on and evaluate the project by presenting an oral report to the class and inviting community people who have been involved in this or other projects. The students describe the results of the project, including both successful and unsuccessful aspects. Finally, students are expected to write individual papers that reflect on the project.

Reference

Clawson, M., & Couse, L. (1998, November). Service learning as a teaching strategy in human development and family studies courses. *Family Science Review, 11*(4), 336–353.

Distance Learning, Technology, and Teamwork

Jana Bradley
School of Information Studies, Syracuse University

Introductory Discussion

In distance learning that takes place within a networked, asynchronous learning environment, collaborative learning and teamwork occur very naturally because the medium of instruction—interaction over the Internet—makes it harder for the teacher to be the hub of the class—the center through which all communication flows. Because the students are taking a course from various locations, they must communicate electronically with each other. They do this via email, chat rooms, bulletin boards, and special sites where they can post their work for others to see. When team projects are assigned as part of the course, the necessary teamwork takes place, per force, via technology.

Distance learning via asynchronous communication over the Internet can be implemented using a pastiche of applications for email, chat rooms, bulletin boards, and web servers for posting html pages. Increasingly, however, courses that rely on asynchronous electronic communication are using applications specifically designed for online courses. The online course application used here is WebCT.

WebCT (World Wide Web Course Tool), which was developed by Murray Goldberg at the University of British Columbia in Vancouver, has become a popular tool for electronic collaboration. In 1999, WebCT was acquired by Universal Learning Technology (ULT), a Massachusetts company that develops web-based teaching and learning platforms. In the spring of 2000, WebCT reports that their platform is in use at over 1,300 academic institutions and 147,000 courses worldwide. More information about this tool is available on their web site: http://www.webct.com/.

The activity described below is one example of how students can do teamwork in a distance learning situation.

Activity: Creating Web Resources at a Distance

In this semester-long project, students sign up for an independent study course, Librarians in the 21st Century. The students never meet face to face, but they earn independent study credit by completing the course project, which gives them practical experience in knowledge creation. Their task is to build a web-based knowledge resource on the subject of librarianship in the 21st century.

The independent study course has two goals: first, to give the students practical experience in building a web-based knowledge resource, and second, to provide experience in completing a complex team project in a distributed environment—i.e., entirely through electronic communication. Students are assigned roles that are specific to the construction of a web site: project manager, information architect, content editor, indexer, technical coordinator, search capabilities coordinator. More students could be accommodated in this structure if students shared roles. The job of each role coordinator or role team is to get input from the other members of the team and then to develop a plan and implementation process for the activities for which they are responsible. The coordinator posts the plan to get feedback from other members, makes revisions, and then supervises implementation of the plan. This was the theory, anyway. In practice, the coordinators often worked with less structure, while still leading the activities for which they were responsible.

The teams tend to start slowly and often work tentatively for a while. The difficulties they encounter as a distance team parallel the problems that teams in a face-to-face environment also encounter, with the added burden of learning how to collaborate electronically. It is useful to encourage open discussion of the problems of electronic teamwork and work strategies to ameliorate the difficulties. As in most online distance learning experiences, it is important to make expectations clear, including the workload per week and the mechanisms of accountability.

Instructions for the Instructor

The activity described occurs as the principle activity of a group independent study, and so the project chosen by the instructor needs to be one that, although complex, can be accomplished by the students mostly on their own, with coaching from the instructor as needed. For an instructor to undertake an activity similar to this, he or she should choose an appropriate project addressing specific content learning goals; however, in addition, the instructor should specifically foster electronic collaborative learning. Since the work takes place via electronic communication, it is important that all students in the class have a basic familiarity with the tools they will use—in this case, with WebCT and with html markup language.

To start such an independent study, an instructor picks an appropriate topic and makes the independent study opportunity known to students. Appropriate entry criteria, such as familiarity with technology, can be established. The instructor decides on the level of structure to be determined in advance, and on the role the instructor will play. In the project described here, the instructor, after setting up the initial structure, was available as a coach, but in general did not take an active part in the discussion, and in fact, monitored it very loosely, checking in only every seven to ten days and relying on the students to ask for help via email when they needed it. The initial task structure will depend on the project and also on the specific learning goals the instructor has set for the students in regard to electronic collaboration. Electronic get-acquainted activities are useful, and almost any face-to-face activity can be creatively adapted. My favorite is "two truths and a lie," where students post three statements about themselves, two of which are true and one of which is a lie. The class then attempts to guess the false statement. The WebCT course environment also supports individual student web pages, on which students can post their pictures, some information about themselves, and lists of their favorite links.

Set-Up and Materials

Although teamwork in an electronic course environment can be done simply via the Internet, WebCT is ideal for setting up teamwork at a distance. One does not need to be a "techie" to use this application, which includes bulletin boards, listservs, chat rooms, and shared server space to post html documents. It is ideal to have a number of electronic communication options available for the students and interesting to see how they evolve in using them. For example, it is possible to schedule chat sessions, in which the whole group gathers at a specified time. Scheduling a group of distance students that are located across the country and internationally is difficult, however, and students in this project wanted the freedom to schedule synchronous discussion as they felt the need. Another aspect of set-up concerns the ability to limit specific communication media to certain groups. Although the particulars will depend on the applications used, it is helpful to give subgroups their own bulletin boards, access to chat rooms, and file space for sharing files. Students will also have to learn the mechanics of how to share their material with others and how to limit it for viewing just by the instructor or by a specified group. Again, these details vary with the application used.

Time Frame/Schedule

The students work together for one semester on this task. For any complex task, dividing it into smaller pieces with associated deadlines is important. Who sets these deadlines depends on the learning goals of the instructor. Some instructor guidance is useful, and in this project there was an assessment and feedback scheduled about halfway through. However, the partition of the project into its component parts, and the setting of related deadlines, was left to the students, much as it is in many group projects where students can meet face-to-face.

Follow-Up and/or Assessment

No paper work is turned in for this project as everything is posted on WebCT. For grading electronic work, the instructor currently uses a split screen, having the student's work on the left side of the computer monitor and a word processing document on the right side in which comments are entered. Some online course environment applications have built-in ways to enter annotations on electronic work, as will new versions of WebCT. The assessment for this independent study is done both at an individual and a group level. The completed project is assigned a grade, which is given to all students and is approximately half of each student's total grade. The individual portion of the student's grade is again divided in half, with half reflecting the student's work in the collaborative process, including the student's role as coordinator and discussion participant, and half reflecting the assessment of the content that the student produced.

Education:
Strategies of Teaching

Mara Sapon-Shevin
Teaching and Leadership, Syracuse University

Introductory Discussion

The activity that is described in this example is part of a course titled Strategies of Teaching. Undergraduates take this course in the Inclusive Elementary and Special Education Teacher Preparation Program that prepares students to teach in heterogeneous, inclusive classroom settings. The course is part of a block of methods courses that combines in-class work and field placements in local elementary schools.

One of the major goals of the course (and the program) is to prepare students with the skills, attitudes, and knowledge they will need to work well with diverse groups of students. Although the primary focus of the program is on preparing students to deal well with students who have been identified as having special educational needs, the term inclusive extends beyond issues of disability to encompass a broader range of diversities, including race, class, gender, ethnicity, religion, and sexual preference.

Activity: Jigsaw on Diversity

How can teachers be responsive to the wide range of differences in their classrooms? What are the occasions on which issues of diversity will become salient? How can teachers help their students learn about diversity issues, introducing those topics through the curriculum and daily classroom practices? This activity is designed to help students learn about a range of student diversities and to engage in problem generating and problem solving behaviors relative to those differences.

Students have previously been divided into "home groups," heterogeneous groups of five or six students who remain together for various projects throughout the semester. The activity involves the book *Common Bonds: Anti-Bias Teaching in a Diverse Society* by Deborah A. Byrnes and Gary Kiger. Every student is required to read the introduction to the book as well as Chapters 7 (Integrating Anti-Bias Education) and 8 (Diversity in the Classroom: A Checklist). Each group is then assigned a particular chapter from those remaining. Each of these chapters addresses another kind of diversity: race, ethnicity, and culture; religion; ability; class; language; and gender. Students are required to come to class with evidence that they have read their assigned chapter (underlining, Post-its, marginal notes, etc.).

Instructions for the Instructor

1. Students are placed in their home groups, and each group is given several large pieces of poster paper as well as markers.

2. Each group is given half an hour to produce the following:

   A poster of key points from their chapter

   A list of dos and don'ts relative to their aspect of diversity

   A two-minute role play to be performed twice, once showing a teacher being insensitive or thoughtless about their aspect of diversity and once showing the teacher being sensitive and thoughtful in that same situation

3. The instructor circulates from group to group, making sure that all students are involved and that students are clear about the task and time frame. The instructor makes sure that the students have appointed a timekeeper and a reporter from each group and assigns roles to all students in the role play.

4. When all groups have completed the task, the class is reassembled, and each group shares their role play, their key points, and their list of dos and don'ts. Students then engage in a discussion about the information presented, raising questions for the presenting group's response.

5. Have students hang their posters on the walls where other groups can consult them.

Time Frame/Schedule

This activity takes about two and a half hours total (15 minutes for organization, 30 minutes in small groups, and about an hour and 45 minutes for presentation). If class meets for a shorter period of time, the group work and presentation work could occur on two separate days.

Follow-Up and/or Assessment

This activity occurs before students go into their field placements in classrooms. One of their assignments while in the field is to conduct a community and diversity analysis in which they observe and report on the ways in which the teacher, curriculum, and pedagogy in the classroom are responsive to various kinds of student diversity. They are asked specifically to draw on what they learned from the jigsaw activity in class when conducting their analysis.

Reference

Byrnes, D. A., & Kiger, G. (Eds.). (1996). *Common bonds: Anti-bias teaching in a diverse society* (2nd ed.). Wheaton, MD: Association for Childhood Education International.

Engineering:
Teamwork in the Lab

Hiroshi Higuchi
Mechanical & Aerospace Engineering

Charles Howell
Consultant on Technical Communication
Syracuse University

Introductory Discussion

Teamwork is important in many facets of education. It plays an especially significant role in projects designed to develop communication skills, and team activities provide multiple opportunities for students to practice these skills. While other learning formats require students to communicate only once, usually at the end of a unit (for example, on a test or exam or in a lab report), team projects build continuous communication into all phases.

Communication skills have been a main focus for engineering education in the last decade. Industry, educational leaders, accreditation agencies such as ABET (Accreditation Board for Engineering and Technology), and government agencies such as NASA (the National Aeronautics and Space Administration) and NSF (the National Science Foundation) have all identified written and oral communication skills as an important component in professional success in the various engineering fields, and have sought ways to introduce those skills into the engineering curriculum.

Activity: Team Projects in an Undergraduate Laboratory Course

At Syracuse, team projects are an integral part of laboratory courses in several of the engineering disciplines. MAE 315, the lab in mechanical and aerospace engineering, is one of several courses that has recently been redesigned to use teams to develop communication skills in innovative ways.

Students sign up to form teams at the outset of the course and remain in them for the entire semester. Members of the team cooperate in carrying out laboratory exercises designed to familiarize them with electronic instrumentation and mechanical equipment, experimental procedures, and methods of data collection. Because of the complexity of these tasks, students cannot complete the experiments unless they work together to understand the instructions, master the underlying concepts, and carry out the prescribed activities with the appropriate safeguards.

Set-Up and Materials

Three laboratory reports are assigned over the course of the semester. The format of these reports is varied in such a way as to exploit team synergies and expose team members to different aspects and problems of communication.

First report: Individual. The first report is composed individually, with each team member turning in a separate report based on data collected in common. Students are encouraged to discuss their data and data reductions, but they are required to write on their own. This procedure avoids a common problem in grading team projects— how to assign a grade that reflects individual contribution and collective achievement. Each team member gets an individual grade for the lab report, but the grade also reflects the team's mastery of procedure, accuracy in data collection, and overall understanding of the goals of the experiment and the principles it was intended to illustrate. The instructor can easily ensure that the writing has been done independently. The instructor can make a preliminary assessment of abilities and efforts of individual members to help subsequent advising. Students are provided detailed written feedback, and at this point they are encouraged to discuss their work with colleagues.

Second report: Collaborative. The second report is written collectively: The team members turn in one report and receive a single grade, unless they turn in a written request that one member's contribution be treated differently. They are encouraged to meet together during or after the experimental phase of the project to plan the composing process cooperatively. At this meeting, they may talk through different sections of the report, such as the introductory section that lays out the theoretical background of the report or the discussion section in which they analyze the significance of the data. They are encouraged to divide up discrete tasks that can be carried out most efficiently by individuals—for example, formatting data for presentation in an appendix, or writing a description of the experimental set-up and procedure. After individual assignments are carried out, the teams meet again to coordinate their efforts: read what other team members have written, make whatever editorial changes are needed for stylistic consistency, compile the parts of the report into a single format, and proofread for errors in spelling and grammar. The overall process is intended to teach students who have uneven levels of technical understanding and different strengths and weaknesses in communication skills to find ways to coordinate their efforts in order to produce a single coherent written product. The process is designed to reflect, in a relatively nonthreatening format, the more urgent demands of cooperation in the workplace.

Third report: Group presentation. The third report is delivered orally to an audience that includes the instructor, teaching assistants, and, if the presenters agree, members of other teams as well. Each student is required to speak; the content and format of the report are sufficiently complex to make this possible. For example, one team member provides an overview of the report, introduces the other members, and summarizes the conclusions of the report in a closing statement. The instructor poses two kinds of questions about the content of the report: questions that are intended to test individual members' active participation during the lab and understanding of the material they or their teammates have presented, and questions that are designed to stimulate creative thought by requiring reinterpretation of experimental results. Questions of the first kind are addressed to specific team members; questions of the second kind are addressed to the team as a whole.

Throughout the semester, the importance of communication skills in professional development is emphasized in lectures and discussions, and students are reminded of the role teams can play in allowing them to practice and refine those skills, as well as in helping them to master the technical principles that the experiments are designed to illustrate.

Time Frame/Schedule
Students complete these three laboratory reports over the course of the semester.

English and Textual Studies: Small Group Technique for Writing/Reading Papers

Patricia Moody
English and Textual Studies, Syracuse University

Introductory Discussion

The seminar method of paper writing/paper reading is a technique that involves cooperation among an informed, concerned, and sharing group of people. It enables each member of a seminar group to receive an abundant amount of individualized attention on a paper that he or she is in the process of writing. This close attention, it is hoped, will help students to create a polished piece of writing that they will be very satisfied with and that others will take pride in having helped to produce.

The seminar method also enables each group member to hone his or her editorial skills. By helping other people to write well, students sharpen their own writing skills, so that they, too, may benefit from the advice they give. In short, the seminar method is what writing is all about: making ourselves understood to others who wish to understand us.

Activity: The Seminar Method

This technique may be used in class either occasionally or on a regular basis, but it is important to prepare the students carefully for the process this activity entails. First, the class should discuss and decide upon the traits that they will be looking for in each paper. They might include the paper's organization, adequate development of supporting paragraphs, strong introductory and concluding paragraphs, well-developed examples, and mechanics. The focus of the writing task may determine other characteristics that are important for a particular assignment.

The instructor should then divide the students into groups of fives. Each student will have a particular role, and students will rotate roles as they proceed through the papers. For example, a different student is the discussion leader for each paper. The diagram on the next page shows the rotation process.

Set-Up and Materials
Students must bring in five copies of their paper, one for each person in the group. Each student should prepare a seminar worksheet for each paper that he or she is reading. These worksheets are described below. The class should also discuss the process of how to give effective advice, criticism, and suggestions to other students (see diagram). Their responsibilities as discussion leaders and seminar group members are described in the worksheets that follow.

Time Frame/Schedule
There are several ways to do this activity. Depending upon the length of the papers and the class time, the students may read, fill out their worksheets, and discuss the papers during class. Another approach is to have the students review the papers and fill out their seminar worksheets outside of class and then use class time just for group discussion of the papers.

Follow-Up and/or Assessment
For a seminar assignment, students should submit:

To the instructor:

- Rough draft of their assignment
- Finished draft of the assignment accompanied by: a) discussion leader's critique; and b) seminar group members' worksheets.
- Response to the seminar method, if required, and how the group discussion affected their rewrite.

To discussion leaders:

- Seminar worksheets on student's assigned traits for each paper

To the author of the paper:

- A critique

The Seminar Method—Diagram of Rotation Process

Writer→ Reader↓	A	B	C	D	E
A	———	3	2	1	DL
B	DL	———	3	2	1
C	1	DL	———	3	2
D	2	1	DL	———	3
E	3	2	1	DL	———

Discussion Leader (DL)   Leads the discussion, summarizes the critique

Group Members (1, 2, 3)   Read paper for assigned traits, give oral report

Author (———)   Listens for meaningful feedback

Worksheet for Seminar Participants

Writing your seminar worksheets can be an exercise in aggressive assault or an experiment in passive pussyfooting. The first will alienate and discourage the author; the second will give too little information to be of any help. You must, instead, give an assertive assessment of the writing you have read.

Your comments will be directed to the author of the paper that you are reading. You, as writer of the seminar worksheet, must encourage the author, making him or her see the strengths of what has been written. But you must also indicate the weaknesses which reduce the paper's effectiveness. Watch your tone very carefully: A tone of condescension can be as offensive as one of abuse. Write in your most effective "you-attitude" style, for the major purpose of your worksheet is to make the writer see your points and to accept your assessment.

Your assessment should derive from your close analysis of the paper. Your seminar worksheet (and oral report) should include the following three areas of comment:

- *Strengths.* Focus on that aspect (of the specific trait that you are reading for) which is best handled by the paper. Focus means not merely citing that such-and-such is well done, but a brief description of how and why such-and-such is well done, giving examples. In short, this means explaining what this trait's strongest asset is.

- *Weaknesses.* Focus on that aspect (of the specific trait that you are reading for) which is most responsible for undercutting the paper's effectiveness. Tie this to an explanation of how this weakness works against the overall impact of the paper. Smaller weaknesses should also be mentioned and explained, though not in as much detail.

- *Overview.* Weight the strengths and the weaknesses (of your specific trait) and determine which carries more force. Is this trait weak, with a few strengths, or strong, with a few weaknesses? Give at least two concrete suggestions for improving the weak areas.

At the top of the seminar worksheet, include the following information:

- Your name

- Your trait

- Name of discussion leader

- Name of paper's author

- Date of discussion

Worksheet: Responsibilities of the Discussion Leader

As discussion leader, you are responsible for leading the discussion of one paper and preparing a written critique of that paper. Specifically, your role includes the following tasks:

- Prior to the discussion, carefully consider each of the assigned traits so that you know this paper inside out. You must be able to speak about each trait, though you will probably not have to.

- On the day of the discussion, begin with a few introductory remarks (not a summary!) including an identification of the author and the subject of the paper. Start the oral reports by calling on the group member who has trait #1.

Hurry those who take too long by requesting a summary of important points. Time is limited, so interrupt if a report goes beyond three minutes.

Based on these worksheets, your own notes, and the group discussion, prepare a critique in which you evaluate the paper for which you were discussion leader. Your audience is the author of the paper. You must establish yourself as intelligent, perceptive, and considerate—someone the author will want to listen to and believe. This credibility is the ultimate goal of your critique. Your critique of the paper must indicate its strengths, weaknesses, and an overall impression. Encourage the author, but be honest. Give your critique and all of the seminar worksheets to the author.

At the end of all the oral reports, summarize the strengths and weaknesses of the paper. Then collect all of the seminar worksheets. Be open-minded to other points of view. If, however, a report has been intemperate or immoderate, let it be known that you disagree with it. For example, if someone criticizes the organization of a paper, missing what you perceive as an effective organizational pattern, tactfully say so.

If someone is absent, give his or her oral report.

Worksheet: Responsibilities of a Seminar Group Member

As a seminar group member, you will look carefully at a specific, assigned trait for a paper and prepare a brief seminar worksheet on it. Your worksheet comments should help to increase the author's awareness of his or her strengths and weaknesses as you share them first as the basis for your brief oral report and then as a permanent written record of your response to what the author has written. Specifically, your tasks include the following:

- Carefully read each paper to be discussed.

- Carefully review your specific assigned trait, which will change for each paper.

- Give an oral report lasting two and one-half to three minutes. Begin your report by stating the trait you are discussing. Then give a general statement that summarizes and describes your findings.

- Continue your report by providing concrete support for your statements. Refer to specific examples in the paper. Know precisely to what features you are referring, citing specific pages, paragraphs, sentences, etc.

- End your report with specific recommendations.

- As you prepare the worksheet on your trait, also review the paper for the other traits, in case you wish to add anything to the discussion about them.

- Prepare a seminar worksheet on your trait and turn it in to your discussion leader at the end of the discussion. Your perception and discussion will form the basis for the discussion leader's critique of the paper.

Fine Arts: A Team Project to Perform an Artistic Happening

Sandra Chai
Fine Arts, Syracuse University

Introductory Discussion

In addition to the usual exams and paper, students taking FIA 448 are required to participate in a group project that is perhaps more specific to the course (formerly titled Surrealism and Related Movements) than most group projects. Each group of five or six students plans a "happening" to be performed near the end of the semester as a climactic event. In more than one instance, a group worked so well together that they continued to meet as a group to study for the final exam. Most students are new to the idea and experience of performing. They are reassured that the group is also there for support, and in the planning stage, each group is expected to find a role or task for each member with which he or she will be comfortable. For example, a group having an international student whose English was not good assigned him a nonspeaking role; he was adorned with and held certain Surrealist objects.

In the words of Allan Kaprow, an artist and latter-day planner of happenings:

> A Happening is an assemblage of events performed or perceived in more than one time and place. Its material environments may be constructed, taken over directly from what is available, or altered slightly; just as its activities may be invented or commonplace.... It is art but seems closer to life (*p. 11, Pasadena Art Museum*).

Activity: Happenings—A Surrealist Group Experience

The purpose of the assignment is 1) to attempt to use Dada and Surrealist methods to understand their attitude toward life and art—an attitude that cannot be grasped solely from lectures, and 2) to work through and participate in a meaningful yet enjoyable group learning experience.

Instructions for the Instructor: Group Selection

The groups are determined by chance, as chance was used as a creative tool by both Dadaists and Surrealists. The instructor puts each student's name on a slip of paper, folds it, and places all of the wads in a bag. The names are drawn at random for the groups. The instructions given to each group reveal the rationale behind the assignment as well as the procedure and means of assessing performances and assigning individual grades.

Set-Up and Materials: Instructions to the Groups

As explained, your groups were determined by chance. Anything that affects your group is, was, or will be similarly determined by chance. For example, the number of members in your group (five or six) was part of the chance selection process, and there are advantages and disadvantages with either number. The combination of personalities, abilities, creativity, and motivation depends on chance—the luck of the draw. The success of the group depends on this chance combination, as well as group effort and cooperation. Performance dates are also assigned by chance.

First Tasks

- Prepare by reading (see also bibliography and books on reserve):

  Allan Kaprow, exh. cat., Pasadena Art Museum, 1967 (excerpt).

  Michael Kirby, ed., *Happenings* (excerpts):
    Allan Kaprow, statement
    Allan Kaprow, "Coca Cola, Shirley Cannonball"
      (script and production)
    Robert Whitman, "Flower" (production)
    Claes Oldenburg, statement

- Exchange phone numbers and email addresses with your group members.

- Decide on a group leader or co-leaders who will do the telephoning and coordinating.

- Arrange a time to meet and begin to plan your happening as soon as possible.

- You will need a name for your group. Some past examples (a couple derived by chance methods): Perverted Placenta Grows Death of Swimming Blue Octopi, The Labyrinth, Why Not?, 13210, Copper the and apple in unum (a.k.a. eggs).

Sources for Happening Ideas

Class notes, course texts, the above specified excerpts, books on reserve, additional articles or books that you discover, etc. Kaprow, for example, identifies six different types of happenings; one of those may suit your collective group personality better than another. You might also combine formats.

Tips: It is a good idea for each individual to make note of ideas as he or she does the reading, and then pool ideas during group meetings.

What You Should Use or Keep in Mind as You Plan Your Happening

- Dada and Surrealist imagery. Example: motifs, themes, and iconography (symbolism) used by the Dadaists or Surrealists, such as fish, eyes, eggs, umbrellas, sewing machines, masks, etc.

- Dada and Surrealist history. Take a cue from famous events that have already taken their place in the annals of modern art history. Example: you may adapt ideas from the 1920 Cologne or the 1921 Paris manifestations, the 1938 Surrealist Happenings, etc.

- Dada and Surrealist techniques and characteristics. Example: the use of chance techniques, automatic techniques, bruitisme (within reason), simultaneous activities, etc. Any of the arts may be involved.

- Make lists during your initial brainstorming sessions.

Time Frame/Schedule

Aim for a 20-minute happening (not including set-up and cleaning up). You should rehearse and time your happening. Criticisms of previous happenings include "too long" and "not enough activity or action."

Limitations

- No excessive noise.

- No excessive mess. We should aim for "dry" happenings: no wet, sloppy materials, please (unless they can be used as part of an outdoor happening). Any necessary CLEANUP after the happening is part of each group's task.

- No pornography. Despite the Freudian sexual orientation of much Dada and Surrealist subject matter, it was usually discreetly and cryptically presented via symbolism.

Violation of these limitations entails risk of forfeit (i.e., a grade of "0").

Follow-Up and/or Assessment

Your individual grades will be an average of:

- Class rating of each group on a scale of 1 to 10

- Within-group (anonymous) rating on a scale of 1 to 10

- Instructor's rating (I will look for imaginative and creative use of Dada/Surrealist motifs, techniques, philosophies, etc.) on a scale of 1 to 10

Reward

The happenings are competitive. Not only will the winning group receive the highest grades, but they will also be taken out for a pizza at the Varsity.

Neo-Dada/Neo-Surrealist Happenings
Class Evaluations

Please rate each group as a whole from 1 to 10 with 10 being the best rating.

Group #_____ Title _____

Rating:

Additional comments on group or individuals:

Neo-Dada/Neo-Surrealist Happenings
within-Group Evaluations

Group #_____ Title _____

1. Please rate the members of your group from 1 to 10 with 10 being the best rating. (This will be strictly confidential.)

2. More specifically, did any group member do more than his or her share or less than his or her share?

3. In what ways did your project fulfill the criteria for a Neo-Dada or Neo-Surrealist Happening?

4. What do you feel were the goals of the project?

References

Pasadena Art Museum. (1967). *Allan Kaprow.* An exhibition sponsored by the Art Alliance of the Pasadena Art Museum, Pasadena, CA.

Kirby, M. (Ed.). (1965). *Happenings: An illustrated anthology.* New York, NY: E. P. Dutton.

Health and Exercise Science: Team Research Report

Jay Graves
Health and Exercise Science, Syracuse University

Introductory Discussion

The course, Research Problems in Exercise and Sport Science PPE 693 (also cross-listed as EDU 791 and EDP 791 Advanced Seminar in Quantitative Techniques), serves as an advanced seminar in quantitative techniques for graduate students. It is a continuation from the previous semester of Current Literature in Exercise and Sports Science (PPE 606). A major objective of the first semester is preparing a research proposal. During the second semester, the students take a research proposal and develop some data to test the hypothesis, using quantitative methods that are taught in the course. Because the course is cross-listed, not all students have taken the previous semester of Current Literature in Exercise and Sports Science.

Activity: The Team Research Report

Students review the current literature on a specific topic in their discipline to develop a research problem. The research report may be an extension of a previously developed research proposal from PPE 606, or students may propose a research proposal in their own area of specialization.

Development of the research report involves the synthesis of data sets to test the stated hypothesis(es). The research report must be written as a research article formatted according to the instructions for publication in a peer-reviewed journal. The report must include:

- An introduction leading to a statement of the problem with appropriate literature citations

- A sufficiently detailed description of the methodology

- A presentation of the results including appropriately labeled tables and figures

- A thorough discussion of the results and conclusions

- A bibliography

Set-Up and Materials

Students ideally work in groups of four to complete their research reports. Each student has a particular role:

- Project leader

- Statistical consultant

- Data technician

- Senior editor

The project leader organizes the meetings and oversees the entire process. The statistical consultant develops the statistical models for analyzing the data. The data technician comes up with the data set that the statistical consultant uses. Each person on the team writes part of the report. The project leader, for example, writes the introduction, the statistical consultant writes the methodology, and the data technician describes the results. The role of the senior editor is to write a discussion of the results and conclusion and also to edit the entire report for format and consistency.

The instructor determines the teams and provides the recommendations for roles and responsibilities, generally giving a student who is strong in statistical analysis but weaker in leadership the opportunity to develop his or her leadership skills by serving as project leader. However, the students can also negotiate among themselves or even rotate roles. Each team may work a little differently.

The class actually meets in a computer cluster; during the semester the students learn the practical application of quantitative research techniques for all graduate students in the School of Education.

Time Frame/Schedule

The students work in teams for approximately half of the semester. They generally have one day of class time to work as a team; the remainder of the time teams must set up their meetings outside of class.

Follow-Up and/or Assessment

During the semester, small informal evaluations are done as students go through the actual process of developing the report and presentation, and some issues or problems may be discussed in class. The statistical strategies chosen to analyze specific data are often used in class as examples to support the various types of data analyses covered. The reports and presentations are given at the end of the semester and are evaluated then. Students also do an evaluation of the participation of the other group members.

Higher Education: Team Teaching a Book

Joan N. Burstyn
Higher Education, Syracuse University

Introductory Discussion

The course HED 605, The American College and University, provides graduate students with an overview of the way that American colleges and universities have evolved. The course helps students develop an understanding of how race, class, and gender have impacted higher education in the United States and how new technologies have changed colleges and universities in the last 200 years. The course also gives students an opportunity to explore a contemporary issue from an historical and analytic perspective.

The team activity that is described here gives students the opportunity to experience working together in a group, doing historical research using primary sources, making an oral presentation, and also assessing the quality of work that they did. By being divided into groups, students are also exposed to an indepth presentation by those in another group on one or two additional books that they have not studied.

Activity: Read and Teach

Depending upon the number of students in the class (usually 20–29), the class is divided into two or three groups to read a book and then teach it to the class, expanding on some issues in the book using historical research of their own. Students may read Walter P. Metzger's *Academic Freedom in the Age of the University*, Ellen Condliffe Lagemann's *The Politics of Knowledge: The Carnegie Corporation, Philanthropy, and Public Policy*, or Carl T. Rowan's *Dream Makers, Dream Breakers: The World of Justice Thurgood Marshall*.

Once the students have established their teams, they are responsible for reading their book. Each group then decides how they will teach their book to the rest of the class. The students usually have three hours for the presentations. They must use innovative methods to engage the class with the materials. Each group must present information about their book so that others in the class may understand the issues covered in it. Each group also introduces the class to related literature or source materials that its members have read for their individual assignments.

In addition to the group project, individual members of the group are required to investigate one or more issues raised in the book by reading more secondary literature or by studying primary sources relating to Syracuse University (or, with permission of the instructor, relating to another institution). Individuals may, if they wish, examine different time periods from the ones covered by the book.

The students develop unusual and creative ways of teaching their book to the class. For example, students have done a live enactment of Thurgood Marshall presenting the case for Brown versus the Board of Education before the Supreme Court. Others have presented videos of the time and cases. Other students have taught the class how the Carnegie Corporation made decisions during different time periods. They gave letters to the class purportedly written by people asking for funding, and the students, representing members of the Carnegie Corporation board, had to decide whether or not to fund the request, based on the criteria the Carnegie Corporation used during that particular time period. The students then had to justify why they funded or rejected the request.

Set-Up and Materials

To determine the teams, the instructor tells the students a little about each of the books; the students then select their own groups.

To prepare the students for the historical research involved in these projects, the instructor teaches the skills of historical research. She also takes the class to Bird Library (the university library) to show them how to access archival records. The instructor is available to help the students if they encounter any problems.

Follow-Up and/or Assessment
Each group must also develop its own evaluation of the presentation. After the presentation, group members collect all the evaluations, use them to draw up their own evaluation of their work, and turn them in. They also hand in one brief account of how the group went about its work and the group's assessment of how successful its class session was, as well as the basis on which it has made this assessment. Students receive both a group grade and an individual grade on the project.

References

Lagemann, E. C. (1992). *The politics of knowledge: The Carnegie Corporation, philanthropy, and public policy.* Chicago, IL: University of Chicago Press.

Metzger, W. P. (1961). *Academic freedom in the age of the university.* New York, NY: Columbia University Press.

Rowan, C. T. (1993). *Dream makers, dream breakers: The world of Justice Thurgood Marshall.* Boston, MA: Little, Brown.

Management: Reading Challenging Texts in Law and Public Policy

Sandra Hurd
School of Management, Syracuse University

Introductory Discussion

The introductory law course in the School of Management is designed to develop students' understanding of the ways in which the legal system influences management decision-making. Teams are used in the classroom to promote student learning, foster collaboration, and create instructional variety. In this exercise, students work in groups to decode a particularly difficult passage of text.

Activity: Understanding Corporate Liability for Crimes of its Agents

The material in the course textbook on corporate liability consists of a case and the following text:

> A corporation may be held liable for the acts of its agents. Even low-level employees can, under certain circumstances, commit acts which will result in a corporation's being held criminally responsible. Under federal criminal law, if an employee was acting in the course of his employment and within the scope of his authority, a corporation may subsequently be prosecuted for the employee's acts. A corporation may be prosecuted for a crime that requires specific intent, so long as the corporate agent was acting with the intent to benefit the corporation.

> [Case] For a corporation to be criminally liable under federal law for crimes committed by its agent, the agent must

have acted with the purpose to benefit the corporation if the crime in question requires proof of a specific intent to violate the law.... Many states do not follow the federal rule. They follow the rule proposed in the Model Penal Code that a corporation will not be liable for a felony unless "the commission of the offense was authorized, requested, commanded, performed, or recklessly tolerated by the board of directors or by a high managerial agent acting on behalf of the corporation" (McGraw-Hill Primus, 1992, pp. 164-165).

Embedded in the text are a number of technical terms and concepts to which the students were introduced earlier in the semester, but which individual students usually don't remember in sufficient detail to allow them to make sense of the above passage. However, they are able to sort it out working collaboratively.

After the introduction of the topic, the class is broken down into teams of five students. Each team is given a sheet of newsprint, tape, and a marker. The following matrix is displayed for them, and they are asked to duplicate the matrix on their newsprint and take no more than 20 minutes to fill in the appropriate rules of corporate liability for each box using the text. At the end of 20 minutes, they are asked to tape their newsprint on the wall simultaneously. They are then instructed to move around the room and evaluate the other teams' responses. After the teams have had a chance to do so, the class resumes with a discussion of whose response is most accurate and why. Incorrect responses are discussed to help students understand where they got off track in their thinking.

Matrix

	Strict Liability	*State of Mind*
State		
Federal		

Instructions for the Instructor

The instructor must bring to class newsprint, tape, markers, and a sample matrix to display. The instructor must determine ahead of time what questions he or she is willing to entertain from teams, whether to make those questions and answers available to all the teams, and, if so, how to do so with minimal disruption to the work going on. Although team responses tend to diffuse responsibility for being wrong, the instructor must also plan ahead how to turn incorrect responses into a learning experience without embarrassing or making students who did not get it right feel self conscious. In some instances, it may be advisable to know the institution's expectations about taping material to the walls.

Set-Up and/or Materials

The teams of five students are announced immediately before the exercise. The instructor can simply ask students sitting near one another to work together, have students count off, or put the teams together ahead of time. If teams are used frequently for these types of activities, the instructor may wish to think about the cost and benefits of having the same students work together over time.

Time Frame/Schedule

This exercise is intended for a 55-minute class. It may be adjusted for a shorter period of time by asking students to fill out the matrix before class or by compressing either the time set aside for students to work together or the time for discussion.

Follow-Up and/or Assessment

It is useful to test the success of this exercise by doing a "muddiest point" exercise at the end of class. Instruct the students to complete, anonymously, the following sentence: "What I still do not understand about corporate criminal responsibility is _____." Collect the responses and review them to gauge the class's level of understanding. Return to confusing points at the beginning of the next class, with specific reference to the matrix.

Reference

McGraw-Hill Primus. (1992). White-collar and business crime: Regulation of business through the criminal process. In Whitman & Gergacz, *The legal environment of business* (pp. 164-165). New York, NY: McGraw-Hill.

Management: Planning and Research Projects in Supply Chain Management

Scott Webster
School of Management., Syracuse University

Introductory Discussion

SCM 402 is an undergraduate course that covers supply chain management systems. These include electronic communication, scanning and tracking systems, enterprise-wide transactional systems, material and distribution requirements planning, and supply chain planning.

Students work in teams to complete a group project that consists of two parts: a hands-on ERP (enterprise requirements planning) exercise and an ERP/SCM (supply chain management) research project. In the exercise, teams work together on the design and day-to-day use of an ERP system at the Orange Furniture Company. The system is called Qube ERP. In the research project, each team selects a unique research topic related to either ERP or SCM applications and publishes a web site documenting the results of their research, including links to other relevant web sites.

Activity 1: Hands-On ERP Exercise

Stage 1: Initial Design and Transaction Processing (2 weeks)

The first week is dedicated to initial design. Teams read the case, do a tutorial, and make decisions on the values for three variables that impact the way data are organized and how information can be reported. In the middle of the second week, each team submits a memo that identifies and gives rationales for their design decisions. The second week is dedicated to learning how to transfer data from Excel to Qube, how to enter transactions (e.g., customer orders and shipments, purchase orders, and receipts), and on understanding the impact of transactions on the system. Each team receives a number of Excel data files that contain start-up values for the Qube database; for example, general ledger data, master schedule file data, vendor file data, customer file data, and routing file data. After loading the start-up data, the teams enter transactions related to customer orders and purchase orders. In the middle of the second week, each team submits reports showing company status before and after the transactions and a memo that summarizes how the transactions are manifested. The purpose of the memo is to promote understanding of what is going on in the system: explaining how different transactions impact multiple files requires a sound understanding of the system design and dynamics.

Stage 2: Material Planning (2 weeks)

In the third week, the teams are given a fresh Excel file that contains start-up values for the Qube database to be loaded into Qube. The team views a material requirements plan (MRP) report and makes decisions on orders to release to the shop and purchase orders to release to vendors. The releases are executed by entering the appropriate transactions into the system. In the fourth week, the team develops a material plan based on information in the system and new customer orders. After loading a fresh Excel file that contains start-up values and entering customer orders, teams generate the initial MRP, decide on how the plan should be changed, and enter the changes through appropriate transaction processing. In the middle of the fifth week, each team submits reports showing the impact of their transactions and their MRPs along with a memo summarizing their transactions and justifying planning decisions.

Stage 3: Putting it all Together (4 weeks)

The fifth and sixth weeks are dedicated to understanding what transpired during the earlier weeks to prepare for the last two weeks in which teams will process transactions provided in Excel files, develop an MRP, make decisions on appropriate transactions, process these transactions, and generate and analyze trial posting reports. Trial posting is the first step in closing the financial statements; once discrepancies are reconciled, the financials can be closed and various statements generated. For the last two weeks, teams are given a fresh Excel file containing start-up values and a list of transactions to be processed. The teams load the data into

Qube, make planning decisions, execute transactions consistent with the plan, and prepare to generate summary financial statements. In the middle of the ninth week, the teams submit reports and a memo summarizing their actions. Finally, one week later, after completing the exercise, each team submits a two-page report. The first page is an assessment of the strengths and weaknesses of Qube ERP. The second page contains suggestions for improving the exercise.

To provide students with additional perspectives on the software, business people from industry participate in five classes during the course of the exercise.

Time Frame/Schedule
Activity 1, which is accomplished during the first half of the semester, is broken down into three distinct phases. This strategy provides a clear structure for the teams and is designed to ensure that students have mastered one set of skills before moving on to another.

Follow-Up and/or Assessment
Assessment is built into Activity 1 through the two-page report that is due a week after the exercise is completed in which the teams are specifically asked to provide suggestions for improving the exercise. The instructor will also gather assessment information through student questions about the exercises and the kinds of problems teams have in completing the various components. In addition, specific questions about the exercise are also asked on the mid-semester and end-of-the-semester course evaluations.

Activity 2: ERP/SCM Research Project

In this part of the group project, each team selects a unique research topic related to either ERP or SCM applications and publishes a web site documenting the results of its research. A list of possible topics is provided, for example, ERP or SCM software—assessment of the strengths and weaknesses of one package, comparison of features of two packages, and summary of implementation experience at two organizations.

The instructor provides the teams with detailed written instructions explaining the requirements for each part of the team project.

The instructions include technical requirements and criteria for grading each assignment.

Instructions for the Instructor

This group project requires significant advance planning and work. For Activity 1, the instructor must generate and check multiple data sets that meet the educational goals of the exercise. He or she must also solicit and manage the participation of industry representatives. For Activity 2, he or she must select topics that are manageable in terms of available student research time and institutional resources. The instructor must also prepare detailed explanations of each phase of the project, develop grading criteria, and plan on considerable in-class and out-of-class time for answering students' questions about the project.

Set-Up and Materials

The teams for this project are formed by the instructor. This strategy mirrors a business environment in which employees are assigned to teams rather than selecting their own. For Activity 2, the teams may choose their own topics, but are constrained in their choice by the fact that only one team is permitted to research a particular topic. A premium is therefore placed on early decision-making.

Time Frame/Schedule

Activity 2 is completed during the last half of the semester and builds on the skills learned in Activity 1.

Follow-Up and/or Assessment

As with Activity 1, the instructor will also gather assessment information through student questions about the exercises and the kinds of problems teams have in completing the various components. In addition, specific questions about the exercise are also asked on the mid-semester and end-of-the-semester course evaluations.

Management: Team Research Presentations in Strategic Human Resource Management

Gisela von Dran
School of Management, Syracuse University

Introductory Discussion

O&M 346 is an introduction to organizational behavior required of all students in the School of Management. It examines the influence of organization structure and management practices on individual and group work behavior.

Students work in teams to complete a group project that consists of two parts: a presentation outline/handout with a bibliography of at least 12 sources and a formal class presentation. The students are also required to write a short individual paper about the group project experience. The purposes of the group project are to increase students' knowledge of key organizational behavior topics; improve students' information gathering (research) skills; improve students' ability to work in groups; improve students' meeting, listening, and collaborative writing skills; provide students practice in public speaking and presentation skills; and increase students' knowledge and awareness of group dynamics and processes.

Activity: Organizational Behavior Group Project

Teams for the group project consist of five or six members. Students prioritize six topics selected by the instructor for the semester. The instructor uses this information to match students with the same or similar priorities. In one recent semester, the topics were conflicts and negotiations in organizations, human rights in the workplace, sociotechnical systems: integrating people and machines, drug and alcohol abuse in organizations, the current state of quality circles in practice, and career planning. Students also indicate three times a week when they are able to meet for at least an hour outside of class with team members.

The instructor provides the teams with written instructions for the outline/handout, the class presentation, and the individual team process paper. The instructions for the outline/handout include research requirements and content. Each team must reference a minimum of 12 current sources. Acceptable sources include journals, periodicals, newspapers, books, and electronic databases with publication dates after January 1, 1992. The course textbook may be one of the 12 sources. Sample research sources are provided. These include, for example, *Academy of Management Review, American Sociological Review, Harvard Business Review, Human Resources Management, Journal of Quality and Participation, Organizational Dynamics, Personnel Journal, Training and Development, Business Week, Forbes,* and *The Wall Street Journal.* The outline/handout must contain an introduction, major findings, and a bibliography. The instructions for the class presentation include technical as well as content and organization requirements. Technical requirements include, for example, length and who must participate. The presentation must include an introduction, a body, and a summary. In the individual group dynamics paper, students are asked to address such topics as the roles each person played, what the group did well, problems encountered by the group and who played a major part in their resolution, what the student would do differently knowing what he or she now knows about the particular group, a reasoned assessment of each member's contribution to the group, and any other observations the student wishes to share.

Instructions for the Instructor

The instructor must determine, prior to the semester, which research topics he or she wants the teams to choose from and prepare a handout for students on which to prioritize their interests and list available meeting times. After collecting information on student preferences and availability for team meetings, the instructor must sort students into teams based on that information. The instructor must also prepare detailed instructions for the outline/handout, the presentation, and the individual paper. These instructions should include the criteria on which each assignment will be evaluated. The instructor should schedule particular office hours during the semester in which to work with individual teams who are having difficulty with team process issues. The instructor must also schedule the in-class presentations, making sure that necessary computer and audio-visual equipment are available.

Set-Up and Materials

The teams for this project are set up based on the students' preferences and available meeting times. Although there are numerous ways to form teams, this method has the advantage of assuring that students will have some control over, interest in, and therefore commitment to the topic they are researching, and that they will have some time each week in which they have declared themselves able to meet together as a team.

Time Frame/Schedule

The form on which students indicate their topic preferences and available meeting times is handed out the second week of class. Topics are assigned and teams created during the third week of class. The teams research their topic and work on their outline/handout presentation throughout the semester; presentations are given during the final weeks of the semester. Individual papers are due at the end of the semester.

Follow-Up and/or Assessment

Assessment opportunities occur in instructor meetings with individual teams. The individual student paper on group dynamics is also an effective assessment mechanism; information gleaned from the papers is used to modify the exercise for the subsequent semester. In addition, specific questions about the exercise are also asked on the mid-semester and end-of-the-semester course evaluations.

Mathematics: Cooperative Groups for Problem Solving

Joanna Masingila
Mathematics/Education, Syracuse University

Introductory Discussion

A number of courses in the department of mathematics, such as MAT 112, 117, 118, and 194, are now being taught by engaging students in a type of teamwork/group problem solving. We are using group problem solving because we have found that:

- Group problem solving is often broader, more creative, and more insightful than individual efforts.

- Interaction with others may stimulate additional problems, insights, and discoveries.

- Students can motivate one another to excel and to accept more challenging problems.

- Motivation to persevere with a problem may be increased.

- Socialization skills are developed and practiced.

- Students are exposed to a variety of thinking and problem solving styles different from their own.

- Students learn to depend on themselves and each other (rather than on the instructor) for problem solutions.

- Conceptual understanding is deeper and longer lasting when ideas are shared and discussed.

The philosophy of these courses requires that students in the course—rather than the instructor—must bear the primary burden for constructing mathematical arguments and for providing mathematical explanations.

Activity: Forming Cooperative Groups

During much of each class period, students work cooperatively in small groups to wrestle with problems that challenge them, to develop new and deeper understandings of fundamental mathematical concepts, and to talk about their new ways of thinking. The following are some tips that we have developed for engaging students in teamwork.

Set-Up and Materials

On the first day of class, the instructor will need to cluster students into cooperative groups of about four students each. Since most students will not yet know each other, initial groups can be formed by merely suggesting that four students who are sitting near one another put their desks together for small group work. Students will then be expected to keep working each day with the same group of people until the teacher indicates that it is time for a change of groups (usually every three or four weeks). When the time comes, some instructors find it best to form new groups totally at random. One way to do this is to put a pile of playing cards near the door and to instruct students to take a card as they arrive at class on the day when groups are to be changed. Then those four who have the same card number (for example, seven or two or queen), regardless of suit, form a group. (The instructor will have to take extra cards out of the deck ahead of time so that the appropriate number of groups of four cards remain; for example, if there are 24 students in the class, an instructor might remove from the deck all cards except those from ace through six. This will leave 24 cards, six sets of four cards each.) There may be times when random assignment to groups does not seem appropriate. For example, if there are one or two students in a class who have trouble working together, the instructor may want to assign groups so that these students are separated. Or the instructor may want to arrange groups so that neither the best students nor the weakest students are concentrated in one group. Near the end of the semester, an instructor may choose to ask each student to turn in a list of individuals they would like to work with and may form groups deliberately to include students who have expressed an interest in working together.

Instructions for the Instructor

The role of the instructor in these classes is quite different from more traditional mathematics classes. Rather than preparing a lecture, the instructor is usually responsible for a three-part lesson: 1) providing a brief introduction to the day's activities, 2) circulating about the room while students work in small groups and making appropriate comments to the groups, and 3) leading wrap-up whole-class discussions where various groups share their thinking about the problem and the instructor helps everyone to consolidate their thinking about their work. This type of wrap-up often occurs several times throughout the class period, as well as at the end of each class.

Before students begin work in their groups, the instructor should talk briefly to the entire class, introducing the activity of the day, explaining any new terminology or special instructions, and indicating how this activity fits into the larger context of the course. Note that this introduction is not a time for telling how to solve the problem at hand: Solving the problem is the task of the students in their small groups. Students will probably be frustrated at first with small group work because they are accustomed to being told by their teachers exactly what to do. By contrast, problem solving activities challenge students to do their own thinking, and the instructor's role is merely to introduce the activity and to guide students to discovering their own solutions.

As the instructor circulates around the room while students are working in small groups, the students need to understand that the instructor will play the role of question asker, problem poser, and careful listener, but that the instructor expects them to be the problem solvers and the explainers. The instructor can tell the students over and over that they must be the problem solvers. But they will only believe it if the instructor demonstrates it by his or her actions in the classroom.

- *Don't be an answer giver.* Try not to provide right/wrong judgments or to tell students how to proceed on a problem. If you do, they will always be waiting for you to tell them the next time, instead of thinking for themselves. If students ask, "Is this right?" ask them how they might decide for themselves. Some appropriate replies are "What do your group members think?" or "Can you find another way to verify your answer?"

- *Deemphasize correct answers.* Try to help students understand that you are more interested in depth of understanding, in ability to communicate mathematical ideas clearly, and in reasonable thinking than simply in correct answers. As you move from group to group, avoid asking, "What did you get?" Instead ask questions that require explanation, such as, "Can you tell me what you've been thinking?" or "What strategies have you been using to approach this problem?"

- *Be prepared with appropriate hints.* There is more than one way to solve nearly every problem. When students are stuck, the instructor may need to provide a hint, but the hint should build on whatever progress the group has already made. For example, if students have been experimenting with specific numbers, it might be appropriate to suggest organizing findings in a table so that a pattern may become more apparent. If students are stuck because a problem has very large numbers or seems too complicated, it might be good to suggest trying some simpler cases first. It is usually not appropriate to provide a hint that merely provides students with the first (or a subsequent) step in a problem solution because this is often tantamount to telling students how to solve the problem.

- *Be prepared with problem extensions.* Some groups in the classroom will work faster than others. The experienced instructor helps these students (and eventually all students) to think beyond the task at hand. For example, it is often useful to ask students how they would solve the problem if conditions were changed (numbers different, question different, more constraints, etc.) or to ask them if they can work from their specific solution to a solution for a generalization of the problem.

One of the most important parts of the class is the wrap-up discussion that takes place after small groups have worked on problems. Once again, the instructor must guard against playing too prominent a role. There is no point in telling the class how their groups should have solved the problem. An instructor who does this will find that groups soon have no motivation to work on their own: Why should students struggle to work a problem if they know the teacher will explain it later? The wrap-up discussion should be a session where all groups have a chance to tell what approaches they tried, how successful or unsuccessful they were, and what conclusions they drew from their efforts. The best discussions are those in which the students do most of the talking—comparing approaches, arguing, and trying to convince one another of the validity of their findings. The instructor's role is to orchestrate this discussion so that everyone has an opportunity to participate, so that everyone can hear and understand what others are saying, and so that some closure is reached by the end of the discussion. Although it is important to allow everyone to contribute (even those whose solutions are incorrect), it is also important not to leave students hanging at the end, uncertain what makes sense and what does not. At the end of an ideal problem discussion, students will have reached their own conclusions about the validity of various problem solutions and will have a good sense of how the day's work fits into the bigger picture of the mathematical concepts being studied in the course.

Time Frame/Schedule

This approach can be used during the entire semester, changing the groups periodically as described above.

Follow-Up and/or Assessment

Since the majority of classwork is done in small groups, classwork is assessed and counted as part of the homework/classwork grade. In some of the classes (i.e., MAT 117 and 118), each exam has a group part and an individual part, so students' group work is assessed along with the individual part.

Nursing: Team Clinical Experience

MaryAnn Middlemiss
Chris Harsel
College of Nursing, Syracuse University

Introductory Discussion

The team project described here was used in an acute care course for second degree nursing students, i.e., students who already have a degree in another field and who have returned to college to get a degree in nursing. The project took place during a summer session when these students were halfway through their program. These students were assigned to a high acuity floor at the Health Science Center in Syracuse. Patients on this floor have received renal (kidney) transplants, have trauma, or have undergone various surgeries.

Activity: Nursing Clinical

To prepare for the clinical experience, the eight undergraduate nursing students, clinical faculty, and the graduate teaching assistant (TA) would go to the high acuity floor and talk with the nursing staff, read patient charts, and make assignments for the next day. The clinical faculty and TA selected the best learning experiences, the students were given information about the patient selections, and they chose, sometimes negotiating with each other, their patient care assignment for that week. As soon as patient selection was completed, the students would have two hours of prep time during which they reviewed the medical records and charts, had equipment orientation, met with the family and client, and started initial assessment. The next morning the students had a preclinical conference, codirected by the faculty member and the TA. The faculty and TA would make sure that the students knew what they had to do for the day, helped them set priorities, and knew where and when they needed help. During preclinical conference, each student would review her goals for the day and her plan of care. Preclinical conferences were also a time for clarifying knowledge and integrating knowledge and patient care. These students had two consecutive days of clinical experience, and they cared for the same individual both days.

Instructions for the Instructor

During this experiential learning experience, the TA served as a coach for the undergraduate students. She was a source of support and knowledge and assisted in problem solving for the younger students. The concept of coaching is recognized in theory, research, and clinical education as a method where the coachee and the coach experience mutual benefits. These include challenge, support, decreased anxiety, increased interest, and personal and mutual satisfaction.

The coaching method is based on a component of Bandura's Social Learning Theory (1971). According to Bandura, research conducted within the framework of social learning suggests that virtually all learning resulting from direct experience can occur on a vicarious basis by observing other people's behavior and its consequences. Much of clinical teaching consists of role modeling, and so the undergraduate students had the opportunity to observe the behavior of the graduate student, and to integrate her knowledge, skills, and attitudes into their professional behaviors. The coaching experience created a supportive and collaborative climate for the students.

Set-Up and Materials

See activity description

Time Frame/Schedule

This was a five-week summer intensive clinical. The students spent 18 hours a week in the clinical setting. First they had a two-hour prep the day before. Then they spent two consecutive eight-hour days on the floor.

Follow-Up and/or Assessment

For the undergraduate students, the team of faculty, TA, and eight undergraduates created a supportive, caring, and fun learning environment. The students loved this collaborative team approach. Even the nursing staff was pulled into the team. The students knew that someone (either the faculty member or the TA) would always be available or could direct another student to help.

The patients and their families also liked the team concept. Because there was a student and two instructors, they felt very cared for. The students were able to try many nursing interventions that otherwise no one would have time to do, for example, music therapy, distractions, orientation with demented patients, discussing cards that they had received, etc.

The experience was evaluated by both the undergraduate students and the graduate student. For the graduate student, it was a unique opportunity to develop teaching skills, to create a supportive environment for learning, to initiate strategies for decreasing anxiety for novice learners in a highly stressful environment, and to increase her own knowledge and skills by being with a faculty member who was able to assist her and to role model effective clinical teaching strategies.

Clinical Evaluation

The faculty member and TA did the clinical evaluations together. They would then give them to the students and discuss them. The students could ask questions, possibly challenge the grade, and validate it if they wanted the grade changed.

References

Bandura, A. J. (1971). *Social learning theory*. New York, NY: General Learning Press.

Nutrition and the Hospitality and Food Service Management Programs: Three Activities

Tanya Horacek
Nutrition and Hospitality
and Food Service Management,
Syracuse University

Introductory Discussion

Students majoring in the nutrition and the hospitality and food service management programs at Syracuse University know that much of their future work involves working in teams with a variety of people. The first activity that is described here teaches students about working with different types of people through the Myers Briggs personality indicator. Students learn about different personality types and have an exercise working with them while trying to resolve a budget problem.

The second team activity involves student teams designing a health promotion program. The final team activity described here is a community nutrition education project. In this example, students used the senior dining centers in the university area, but other locations can also be selected. This activity may also be used as a community service project.

Activity 1: Using the Myers Briggs Type Indicator to Develop Dietetic Students' Team Decision-Making Skills

The Myers Briggs Type Indicator (MBTI) is a personality preference indicator that is used to increase self-awareness, but also to enhance understanding and appreciation of individual differences. Once students are comfortable with the basic MBTI theory and their own personality preferences, we work through a couple of case studies to illustrate communication, decision-making, and teamwork principles.

In one exercise, students attempt to solve a problem in the same MBTI type groups. As we start to discuss the solutions each group derived, the students quickly see how each group is distinguishable by certain traits and that the solutions are somewhat unbalanced. They note how easy it is to communicate and how they enjoy talking with people who think like themselves; however, they see that some of the solutions may not be ideal.

We then discuss a method for making more effective and efficient decisions by adjusting for personality preferences. The traditional decision-making model focuses on the steps in the rational decision-making process. The steps in this model proceed as follows: 1) recognizing and defining the problem, 2) identifying alternatives, 3) evaluating alternatives, 4) selecting the best alternative, 5) implementing the chosen alternative, and 6) follow-up and evaluation. This is a good model for making decisions; however, the advantage of employing the Z model on the next page is that it accommodates a variety of individual preferences to problem solving. According to the Z model, individuals with certain preferences will have a greater contribution or sensitivity to two of the four steps. Thus, soliciting input from a group and providing for the input of the individual preferences will result in a more synergistic decision that addresses the needs and preferences of the whole group.

Students then work in mixed, not type-specific, groups/teams of three to four students. They are given an unbalanced budget for a small hospital nutrition and food service department and told to use the Z model to walk them through each step of the process to attempt to balance the budget. The object is to ensure all preferences are purposefully included in their decision-making process. The students are told that it is not the unbalanced budget that is the problem—this is a superficial result of some more specific issues within the system. Since no resources are provided, the students have to make many assumptions and identify what resources they would want to use. The point of the exercise is not for a group to come up with a right answer but to work as a team to ensure they adequately address the problem by using each step in the Z model.

In general, these mixed teams using the Z model generate similar, higher quality, more balanced solutions; however, students always mention that it requires more discussion and debate to get to those decisions.

Instructions for the Instructor

The MBTI is administered and interpreted at an earlier session because it is important that the students be familiar with their own type and the Myers Briggs Type Theory prior to doing these case study exercises. There are numerous options for administering the indicator.

- Provide directions for the students to complete the indicator on their own time and then have them return it with sufficient time so that the results can be scored prior to the basic interpretation session. The basic interpretation session can then be completed in approximately 60 minutes.

- Use the self-score indicator within the basic interpretation session. This basic interpretation session takes approximately 90 to 120 minutes to complete. Many career development centers are able to provide this service.

Set-Up and Materials

Work with a large enough group (at least 20 to 25 students) to see a variety of preferences. Use a room that is large enough and that has moveable chairs so that the group can be divided into smaller work groups

Time Frame/Schedule

The basic interpretation session (if students complete the indicator on their own time) is essential and takes approximately one hour to complete. The case studies and description of the problem solving model takes at least 90 minutes.

Follow-Up and/or Assessment

The outcome of the activity is processed by reviewing what the students had decided they would do for each of the Z model steps. Clarifications are made when the suggestions do not match the step. For example, most groups tend to proceed immediately into the generation of ideas for either cutting spending or increasing revenue. A discussion is often necessary regarding the need to define the problem appropriately, or at least the information they should look at to help them define the problem. If they were a manager, what types of records/information would they need to help them better define the problem (sensing) before generating solutions? We finish the exercise by summarizing how the decision-making model and personality preferences can be considered to improve their own decisions through the conscious input of others with different preferences.

Z Model for Problem Solving

1. Sensing	2. Intuition
• Collect facts	• Understand implications
• Define problem	• Possible solutions
3. Thinking	4. Feeling
• Analyze/evaluate each solution	• Implications
• Pro's/con's	• Effect on people involved
• Gained/lost	

The Z model, the Zig-Zag process for problem solving, is credited to Gordon A. Lawrence (1988) from the Center for Applications of Psychological Type, Gainesville, Florida.

Activity 2: Development of a Health Promotion Program Using Precede-Proceed

This assignment helps students to learn Precede-Proceed, a health promotion planning model, by having them work in teams to sketch a program. This program development process is complex and would typically take a team of people at least six months to apply. Over a period of two months, teams of students work intensively to collect some data and to get a feel for the six steps of the process. Intense interview, library, and Internet research is required and funnels into one draft chapter due weekly. Students select their own teams depending upon their intervention target group interest. Occasionally, instructor assistance for team formation is provided due to student familiarity and assertiveness.

The students learn very quickly that it does not work to simply divide the work; they must work as a team to collaborate because each chapter/step builds upon the previous chapter or step. They need to meet intensively to discuss how 1) they understand each step, 2) to interpret the data they collect and the assumptions they make, and 3) to outline exactly what they want in each chapter of the paper. A draft of each chapter is due weekly, and feedback is provided prior to the submission of the next chapter. Typically, each team member will take a turn for the responsibility of writing a chapter; the more effective teams get feedback from team members prior to the submission of a chapter. Otherwise, a few teams do write each chapter as a group.

The end product is 50- to 60-page document, in which each chapter carefully builds up to the next. Each team presents their proposed program to the rest of the class and to community experts through either an oral presentation or a poster session. The object of their presentation is to sell the need for and the concept of their intended program and to obtain the necessary grant funding.

Instructions for the Instructor
Have the students either read the first few chapters of Green and Krueter's book or a summary chapter about Precede–Proceed. Through an initial lecture, share an example of how the model has been used to set up another program to help them get an idea for how to apply the model.

Set-Up and Materials
No special set-up is required. Formulating the groups can be left up to the students, or the professor may assign them.

Time Frame/Schedule
Students have approximately two months to complete this project.

Follow-Up and/or Assessment
Individual mastery of content is assessed through weekly quizzes. Although a single grade is assigned for the paper, it is up to the team members to decide how the grade is divided. The individual grades are based upon feedback from the students. Each team member evaluates how all team members, including themselves, contributed to the project.

References

Green, L. W, & Krueter, M. W. (1999). *Health promotion planning: An educational and ecological approach* (3rd ed.). Mountain View, CA: Mayfield.

Lawrence, G. A. (1988). *The zig-zag process for problem solving.* Gainesville, FL: Center for the Application of Psychological Type.

Activity 3: A Community Nutrition Education Project

Each semester a site is chosen for the class to do their community nutrition education intervention. This past year, for example, we used the senior dining centers. Since this project is also a service-learning project, we determine how best to serve the community system while giving our students experience in doing a group presentation. The senior dining director informed us of past nutrition education events (to avoid redundancy) and indicated that they needed some satisfaction data collected.

As a full class (or, when the class is bigger, in smaller groups), we designed a simple satisfaction survey that also addressed some of our audience assessment issues. The seven students in this class divided into three teams to work on their group presentation. Each team conducted satisfaction/need assessment interviews in two or three senior dining sites. As the teams collected their data, they then entered it into a master spreadsheet and received a data summary from the sites they visited. From their two or three sites, the students chose one site in which to do their group presentation. They revisit this site often to collect additional audience assessment data. As a team, they develop their group presentation, supporting materials, and evaluation methods based upon their audience assessment and the desired topic. Each team member has a part in the presentation development and delivery.

Instructions for the Instructor

Lecturing about the nutrition education process and making the original contact for the site placement is essential.

Set-Up and Materials
Students typically determine their own groups.

Time Frame/Schedule
Allow approximately two months for the students to complete their research and program development; end the process with group presentations.

Follow-Up and/or Assessment
As part of their evaluation, the students write a self evaluation of how well they worked together to accomplish their objectives. Finally, at the end of the semester, they grade themselves and each of their teammate's contributions toward the project, which the instructor considers when deciding final grades. The overall success of the group presentation depends upon how well students work together as a team to plan and practice their event. Their grade is based upon four parts: the audience assessment, which includes a summary of their research; their presentation outline; the actual presentation; and their evaluation/analysis of the presentation and their process.

Public Affairs: Student Teams and Undergraduate Teaching Assistant Teams

William Coplin
Public Affairs Program, Syracuse University

Introductory Discussion

The introductory public affairs course at Syracuse University, PAF 101, introduces students to the analysis of public policy. Teams are used in two distinctive ways in this class. The students work in teams to practice the skills taught in the course, and the instructor uses a team of undergraduate teaching assistants (TAs) to help run the course. This discussion will give a brief overview of how both teams are used in the first part of the course. Additionally, it will explain how the team of undergraduate TAs facilitates the teams in the course as well as coordinates the implementation of the course.

The first segment of this course is called the Community Link Team Approach (CLTA). The topics in this segment include identification of societal problems, public policies, and players. Students also learn to apply the three components of public policy issues, and they select a public policy topic to study. The CLTA project introduces students to the process of creating public policy and also gets them acquainted with working in teams by participating in an exercise in which they try, for the first time, the skills that are taught in the course. This exercise gives the students a benchmark for where they started in the course.

Activity 1: Plunging into Teamwork

Before the third lecture in this class, students are divided into teams of approximately eight students and are asked to sit together during the lecture where they periodically have team exercises to do. While they sit together, quickie team competitions are also held.

This creates "neighborhoods" during the class. The teams also meet separately five times during the semester. In class the teams are rotated around the room so that one team is not always in the front or another team not always in the rear of the lecture hall.

The CLTA project is the first one that the teams do together, and the CLTA problem is introduced during the fourth lecture. One problem is selected each semester. Problems that have been used in previous semesters include faculty not holding office hours on a regular basis, racial segregation that exists in residence hall room assignments, and underage drinking on campus. The instructor explains the format, hands the class a sample project, and gives students some facts about the chosen topic. Then the groups are sent to various rooms to begin work on the problem. For the next two class periods there is no lecture. Instead, each group goes directly to its assigned room to complete the CLTA assignment. Each group has an assigned TA for support. The TA also gives the team members format guidelines on how the CLTA assignment should be organized.

After the teams have had three team meetings, the next lecture is a CLTA debriefing. The professor goes through the CLTA exercise and presents the policies proposed by all the teams. He asks the students what they have learned about public policy analysis. Next he explains the proper steps for doing public policy analysis: 1) clearly define the problem, 2) identify the causes, 3) develop policies aimed at the problem, and 4) think of feasibility in terms of gaining support from powerful players. Finally, he outlines what is needed for quality team project performance: consensus, support, responsibility, respect, and correct time.

Instructions for the Instructor
This type of teamwork requires a great deal of advance planning. The instructor should think through the entire process, including the time frame, well in advance of starting the project. Expectations and requirements should be given to the students so that they do not spend their time guessing what the instructor wants.

Set-Up and Materials
Note that the teams are set up in advance. This particular activity plunges the teams into a project without a lot of advance preparation; however, each team has a TA to serve as a facilitator. Also,

teams have an assignment to complete during each team meeting, so there is a definite structure for their work. Doing the first activity in this manner forces the students to confront immediately many of the issues that teamwork involves, yet there is a definite structure or safety net for support.

Time Frame/Schedule
For this first activity in the course, students are assigned to teams in the third lecture, and the CLTA problem is explained during the fourth lecture. After the problem is introduced, the teams are sent to various rooms to begin work on the problem and to do the first assignment. The next two classes are team meetings (there is no lecture); lecture five is devoted to debriefing the CLTA exercise. The policies proposed by all of the teams are reviewed and students are asked what they have learned about public policy analysis. They also discuss what is needed for quality team project performance.

Follow-Up and/or Assessment
The grade for this activity is less than 8% of the grade for the entire course. After this activity the instructor should collect feedback from the students so that he or she can fine-tune the process that is being used. Some possible questions are:

- What was your grade on this activity?

- Do you feel that your grade adequately reflects the work you did? Why?

- What did you find valuable in the lecture on instructions?

- How would you improve this lecture?

- What did you find valuable about the CLTA exercise?

- How would you improve this exercise?

Activity 2: A Team Approach to Undergraduate Teaching Assistants

The PAF 101 course that is described above also uses a team of undergraduate TAs to help run the course. The professor selects a team of 12 to 15 students who have previously taken the 101 course and who want to be TAs. As teaching assistants, these students take a class together, PAF 409: Intermediate Public Policy Analysis, and receive a grade for the three credits they earn in PAF 409. The TAs are supervised by the professor and his assistant, and they behave as if they were employees. During the semester these TAs become molded into a team that facilitates the implementation of the course.

At the beginning of the semester, each TA receives a *Teaching Assistant's Manual PAF 101* that describes the approach that is used, gives general assignments for the TAs, and describes staff and lunch meetings, office hours, in-class activities, grading, community service, selecting future TAs, etc. Each TA also has a specific job to do during the course, and the manual describes these jobs: TA Manager, Competition Director, Outside Speaker Coordinator, Newsletter Editor, Community Service Coordinator, Quality Assurance Manager, etc.

Instructions for the Instructor

Setting up a team of undergraduate TAs requires a great deal of start-up work and must be individualized for each particular situation. If you are interested in this type of effort, you may contact Bill Coplin (315–443–3709 or wdcoplin@syr.edu) to obtain a sample *Teaching Assistant's Manual PAF 101* at the price of $5.00 to cover the cost of copying and mailing. Checks should be made out to the Syracuse University Public Affairs Program and sent to: Public Affairs Program, 102 Maxwell Hall, Syracuse University, Syracuse, New York, 13244.

Set-Up and Materials

The set-up for an undergraduate TA program should be individualized according to the needs of each class or program. Each person who uses TAs and sets up such a program will put his or her unique touches to it, though some aspects will be routine. Most faculty find TAs work best when they take a course together and earn credit for their work, rather than receiving cash stipends.

Time Frame/Schedule

This course/TAship lasts for one semester.

Follow-Up and/or Assessment

Each TA in the course is required to submit a semester report that documents the work the TA did during the semester and provides a guide for the next semester's TA. The report must include a self-evaluation and suggested changes in which the student identifies problems and presents solutions. The report also includes suggestions for improving any other aspects of the class.

Sociology: A Collaborative Community Research Project

Arthur Paris
Sociology, Syracuse University

Introductory Discussion

This example of a small research project in sociology illustrates a successful collaboration among students working with a faculty member on a research project that provided an opportunity to apply academic skills and knowledge to a community setting (outreach).

Activity: Team Research Project

The faculty member had received a request to analyze the local Syracuse economy (from 1950 to the present) and investigate connections between its changing economic climate and racial make-up. He recruited three students to work with him on this research project. The these students were all senior sociology majors, had all taken the professor's urban sociology class as juniors, and were serving as course assistants for the course the following year.

For the project, the students collected data and produced an analysis. First, the study examined changes in local demography in both the city and the county from 1950 to the present. The key findings: a decline in population in the city during that period and shifting racial dynamics. Next, the research study linked demographic changes to changes in occupational structure. The key finding: a decline in a higher-wage industrial economy and growth of a lower-wage service economy.

Instructions for the Instructor

To do this type of team research, the instructor needs a project or set of tasks that the students are capable of doing within a semester. The instructor should pick the students carefully to be certain that their skills mesh with the project's needs. There should be a few initial activities to help the students meld together as a team. The professor should spend enough time with the students so that they identify with the project, with each other, and with the faculty member; they should also have a clear understanding of the work that the project involves.

Set-Up and Materials

The students worked together in the department's resource room, which has computers and library size tables. The professor's office was also available for students to use. They kept their materials in the office, on the computer, and in their own files.

The team met with the professor several times a week as a group and also informally with one another. Occasionally the team also met over breakfast.

Time Frame/Schedule

The students worked on this project during one semester. The professor laid out the time frame of the project with the students and met with them on a weekly basis to check on their work and progress. The project was treated as a consultancy since the study had been requested by a client; periodically, the faculty member also met with the client.

Follow-Up and/or Assessment

The faculty member collaborated with the students on a paper about the project (methods and results) which they submitted to the Eastern Sociological Society conference. The paper was accepted, and the students presented it at ESS in March, 1998, where it was well received. In late April they presented their research at the sociology department's Senior Symposium and its Alpha Kappa Delta Honor Society induction ceremony.

Two of the students felt that their experience on this project helped them get jobs with community organizations, one in Syracuse and one in another state.

Writing: Small Group Work in a Writing Class

Nance Hahn
Writing Program, Syracuse University

Introductory Discussion

Writing—written language—is best learned in active, interactive communities. But many students enter their first college writing class hesitant to engage in small-group work, an activity that probably produced mixed results in high school. "The Tray" and "Editing Energizer" provide students opportunities to experiment with two versions of small-group work and, with guidance from their instructor, to reflect on the experience.

Activity 1: The Tray

How can working with a small group enhance each individual's problem solving outcomes? How can diverse student perspectives enrich group creativity? In this exercise, students work together to begin inquiring into these questions.

Instructions for the Instructor

Load a serving tray with 30 to 40 small items. Try to collect a large variety made of a number of different materials, and try to include at least a few items for which the students will not know names. Coins, small tools, pebbles, toys, photos, postcards, nuts, buttons, paperclips, jewelry, shells, computer parts, fruit, writing implements, and scientific, technical, or medical instruments...all these and anything else you can find. Assemble them so that all are visible, although not necessarily in their entirety. Stack or overlap so that everything fits. Cover the tray so that it can be unveiled when the exercise begins.

Set-Up and Materials

Encourage students to stand and gather around the covered tray, and tell them that they will have roughly one minute to look at what is about to be revealed. During the time that the tray is unveiled, they may walk around and move closer, but they may not touch the tray or the items on it, and they may not talk to the instructor or to each other. After the time elapses, cover the tray and ask the students to return to their seats.

Next, ask the students to take out pen and paper and write down as many of the items on the tray as they can recall. When the writing slows down, ask about how many items are on their list. Then ask them to work with a partner, first combining lists, then chatting briefly and writing any new items that they can. At this point most will discover that working with a partner yields more than the sum of their separate lists because the conversation stimulates association and recall. Instruct pairs to collaborate so that groups of four are formed. One or two groups of four may come up with a comprehensive list, at which point you can again unveil the tray and discuss what they see.

Work in groups of four again to invent as many different categories as possible for sorting the items. Compare results.

For the last part of the activity, ask the students to work alone again to write informally for ten minutes about anything related to the tray, its freight, and/or the activity they have just experienced. Let students take turns reading their writing aloud.

Time Frame/Schedule

This activity takes half an hour or perhaps a little longer.

Follow-Up and/or Assessment

In the large group, discuss what the students have observed in the activity. How might it apply to their work in a writing class? How might it be applied to their work in other classes? What are some of the advantages and disadvantages of collaboration for stimulating creativity?

Activity 2: Editing Energizer

Students sometimes resist working in small groups to edit each other's written work, claiming that only the instructor can find and correct errors. Research demonstrates that students best internalize and apply conventions of standard written English when they discover errors themselves, in context. This exercise helps students begin to develop independence and responsibility for the correctness of their own written texts.

Instructions for the Instructor

Plan this exercise for a day early in the semester when students will be bringing a short (no more than two typed pages) piece of writing to hand in. Ask them to bring an original, two copies, and their writing handbooks (for example, Diana Hacker's *A Writer's Reference* or *A Pocket Style Manual* or *The Writer's Brief Handbook* by Alfred Rosa and Paul Eschholz).

Set-Up and Materials

Divide students into groups of three and ask them to take turns reading each piece aloud slowly and carefully. Listeners follow along with copies, and the instructor circulates and acts in a consultative capacity. The group stops whenever a member finds or has a question about a technical control issue such as grammar, punctuation, spelling, capitalization, and the like. Small groups should try to use handbooks to resolve questions as they occur. Observations and unresolved questions should be brought to the large group to be discussed.

Time Frame/Schedule

This activity takes at least an hour.

Follow-Up and/or Assessment

The instructor should model using the handbook to address any remaining unanswered technical control questions. This includes describing each problem, looking it up (even if you do not know its "real" name), and deciding how to apply what the handbook advises.

The instructor should then guide the large group to reflect on "what happened" in the small groups. Students may notice that they brought work they thought was ready to hand in, only to discover that it contained errors in grammar, punctuation, and so forth. They may see that no one in the small group may have been sure of the specific rule or convention needed, but the group together was able to correct the error. Further, they may observe that different group members are tuned in to different kinds of errors—one may be attuned to comma use, another to homonym spelling, another to the nuances of conventions of capitalization. This last recognition can lead to the idea that the large group can work toward developing technical control experts who can be consulted in future editing sessions.

References

Hacker, D. (1997). *A pocket style manual* (2nd ed.). Boston, MA: Bedford Books.

Hacker, D. (1999). *A writer's reference* (4th ed.). Boston, MA: Bedford/St. Martins.

Rosa, A., & Eschholz, P. (1996). *The writer's brief handbook* (2nd ed.). Boston, MA: Allyn & Bacon.

IV

Articles/Resources

Enhancing Performance in Small Groups

R. J. Chesser
School of Management, Syracuse University

One of the most significant trends to emerge in management in the last decade has been the growing use of small groups. More and more, the small group is becoming the most relevant unit of analysis in studying organizations. The reasons for the emergence of the small group are many. As technology becomes more complex and environmental uncertainty increases, some type of collective effort is required to ensure that the relevant knowledge and skills are available. It has become increasingly clear that facilitating effective participation, such as that which can occur in small groups, can generate a sense of ownership that, in turn, enhances motivation, commitment, and performance.

These same forces are active in the academic community. Group-based teaching techniques have become very popular. Students can expect to be a part of many small-group learning communities. They can also expect to be evaluated, at least in part, on how well their groups function. Like employees, it is important that students understand the complex nature of performance in small groups. Beyond promoting learning and higher classroom performance, this understanding will help them demonstrate that they have the ability to work well in groups, which is one of the most important attributes employers look for when hiring individuals whom they consider to have high potential.

The purpose of this chapter is to explore the dimensions of performance in a group setting. Specifically, it focuses on two types of group processes: facilitating performance and limiting performance. It also offers some suggestions on how to increase group effectiveness.

The effectiveness of a group can be represented by the following relationship:

Group Performance =
Individual Performance + Assembly Effect - Process Losses

One way to look at group performance is to equate it to the sum of the individual members' performance. If you did this, you would most likely either understate or overstate group performance. This is due to the next two terms in the relationship: assembly effect and process loss. The assembly effect adds to group performance while process loss reduces group performance. Whether or not a group is more effective than the sum of the individuals in the group is a function of the relative impact of these two opposing terms. Each of the terms in the above relationship is discussed below.

Individual Contributions to Performance

Each member of a group brings knowledge, skills, and a psychological set. The collective knowledge and skills represent the resource base that acts as a constraint on group effectiveness. A group can work together very well, but unless it has adequate resources, it will not be very effective. It is important for the group to have sufficient technical expertise as well as members with good interpersonal and group skills. For this reason, it is important for a group to perform a realistic assessment of its resources. Any deficiency needs to be corrected. This can be done by bringing in new members or training existing members. The psychological set that members bring to a group is more complicated. How motivated are the members? Are they committed to the group and its mission? Much as individual performance is a function of ability and motivation, a group's performance is enhanced when its members are highly motivated.

Assembly Effect

The assembly effect is based on the notion that something positive can happen when people interact. As the number of members increases, the group simply has more resources available from which to draw. By definition, it has more ideas, viewpoints, knowledge, and skills than any individual member. As the group interacts, these resources can increase. One member's comment triggers a new idea in another member. The two ideas result in a third member offering a totally new approach to a problem and so on. In the jargon of group dynamics, this is called synergy. Without interaction, this dynamic could not occur. Technically, synergy is defined as the force that integrates discrete phenomena into organic, dynamic, whole relationships, bringing about behavior that is impossible for the respective components in isolation. In simpler terms, synergy is experienced when the whole is greater than the sum of the parts. In terms of group effectiveness, a synergistic group would be more effective than the sum of the individual members' contributions and would even improve upon the performance of the group's most effective member.

Synergy is a function of the procedures used by the group. The procedures vary by the degree of interdependence, they create among group members. Generally speaking, procedures generating low interdependence yield a small assembly effect. For example, a procedure frequently used by groups is to divide up the total task and assign pieces to individual group members. While this strategy can be efficient in terms of time, it results in minimal assembly effect. The quality of the final product can be no better than the weakest part. Procedures generating high interdependence, such as consensus-making, offer the possibility of a significant assembly effect. Consensus-making encourages unrestricted, face-to-face interaction among group members. If done well, a course of action will emerge to which group members are committed. To promote synergy, group members should not be defensive about their own opinions. Group members should present their views as logically and clearly as possible but be willing to listen to other views. In fact, group members should actively seek out differences of opinion. Members should avoid conflict avoidance behaviors such as voting, coin tosses, and averaging. Members should also not change their minds just to avoid conflict. Underlying assumptions should be explored, and all members encouraged to participate fully.

Much of the literature justifies the use of groups on the grounds that there will be synergy. In reality, groups do not always experience synergy because of the presence of process losses.

Process losses are group dynamics that reduce the effectiveness of a group. They can be sufficiently large so as to offset even the most impressive assembly effect. There is a Catch-22 here. High interdependent procedures that promote synergy also run the risk of process losses. Low interdependent procedures designed to safeguard against process losses generate very little assembly effect. A more appropriate strategy would be to use high synergy procedures such as consensus while minimizing process losses. Some of the dysfunctional processes, such as group think, social loafing, and free-riding, are familiar concepts. There are other process losses that are not so obvious but can account for significant performance problems. These are discussed below.

Process Losses

Process Loss 1: Let's Stop Wasting Time and Get Down to Business

To understand the dysfunctional dynamics associated with this problem, we need to deal briefly with the way groups develop over time. There are two basic issues that groups face. One is the task at hand, and the other is the psychosocial environment. In group dynamics, these two sets of issues are called task issues and maintenance issues.

Task issues. These include such things as setting agendas, establishing procedures, setting objectives, analyzing problems, generating alternatives, evaluating alternatives, and deciding.

Group maintenance issues. These issues, on the other hand, deal with such things as group cohesiveness, influence, leadership, participation, and conflict management. Research into group dynamics suggests that the group maintenance issues must be addressed before the group can effectively focus its attention on the task at hand. Many models of this process have been proposed. A model that many have found useful was developed by Schutz (1958). In this model of group development, members of a group face three issues: inclusion, control, and affection.

- **Inclusion.** When people join a group, the first issue they face is inclusion. This issue focuses around whether or not they are going to be part of the group and how much of themselves they are going to invest in the group. Schutz refers to this as the "in or out" issue.

- **Control.** Once the issue of inclusion is resolved, control then becomes important. This issue has to do with power and influence. How much say are you going to have in the group? How much influence are you going to let others have over you? Schutz calls this the "top or bottom" issue.

- **Affection.** When and if the control issue is satisfactorily resolved, the next issue that surfaces is affection. This issue goes much beyond simply choosing to become part of the group. It deals with commitment. It means choosing whether or not to become emotionally tied to other group members. To Schutz this is the "near or far" issue. Each member of the group must work through these issues to his or her satisfaction. This is purely a personal matter.

The important point is that these issues consume members' energy until the issues are resolved. This means that other concerns, such as problem solving or task accomplishment, are given secondary attention. If a group attempts to focus on task issues before the group issues are resolved, the results will be unpredictable and most likely will lack creativity. For example, Frank's suggestion is given too much attention simply so he will feel part of the group, or Mary's solution is chosen because she has become the most dominant member. Neither of these situations is desirable; both demonstrate how a group can use the task to resolve maintenance issues. A well-functioning group will process suggestions and evaluate alternatives based on merit, not as a way of helping members work through personal issues.

It would be an oversimplification to recommend that a group resolve all of its maintenance issues before it focuses completely on the task. Maintenance issues can surface at any time during a group's life. Most likely what occurs is that individual members switch from one type of issue to the other as the group interacts. For example, in the middle of a discussion of alternatives, control issues could surface for one or more members. Unless other group members are sensitive to the emergence of such issues, the discussion of alternatives could become contaminated with maintenance issues.

It is important to keep in mind that inclusion, control, and affection are individual issues. Each person wants to feel included to some degree and attempts to include others to some degree. The same is true for the issues of control and affection. From the group's standpoint, these issues are resolved when sufficient inclusion, control, and affection behaviors are being exhibited to meet members' needs. When there is either a surplus or shortage of these behaviors, some members' needs are not being met, and maintenance issues surface.

The lesson here is to be a little patient. Before the group gets down to the business at hand, it is better to spend some time dealing with the maintenance issues. It is important to get to know each other. I have seen student groups work together for three hours and at the end still not know each others' names. It would be difficult to feel included in this situation. It is also important to determine how the people feel about being a member of the group. Does someone have reservations about being a member? If so, how can the other members help include them? The small talk at the beginning of a group interaction is generally aimed at inclusion. To many, this is a waste of time. Unless it is excessive, however, it can actually be a time saver if it helps avoid the repeated resurfacing of inclusion issues.

Control issues are very difficult to resolve because they deal with the emotional issues of power and influence. More is said about this later in the chapter in the discussion of leadership and conflict, where it will be pointed out that there are many ways for members to feel influential. One of the helpful things a group can do early in its life is to openly discuss the issue of control. As a general rule, people are more apt to be receptive to influence attempts based on knowledge than they are to attempts based on some arbitrary criterion, such as status. This further supports the premise that it is important to know the other group members. What resources do they bring to the group? Do they have areas of special expertise? The answers to these and similar questions can help group members assign influence in such a way as to facilitate the resolution of control issues. The group also has to maintain an awareness that the control issue can surface at any time.

Because of the difficulty of resolving the control issue, group members frequently do not get to address the issue of affection. The concept of affection in this sense should not be confused with intimacy, although that may occur. The issue has to do with the strength of the emotional ties among group members, a series of dyadic relationships. For example, in a particular group you may feel very close to some members, feel indifferent toward some, and dislike others. It is more important that group members resolve their affection issues than it is that they feel very close to each other. Of course it would be difficult for a group to function well if the members could not stand each other, but it is not necessary that the group be one big happy family. As will be pointed out in the discussion on conflict, total harmony is usually a facade anyway.

Process Loss 2: First, Let's Choose A Leader

A popular myth is that a group has to have a leader. This myth is perpetuated by a failure to distinguish between a leader and leadership. It is true that a group has to have leadership, but this need not be identified with a single person. In fact, attributing leadership to a single person is generally dysfunctional, particularly in regard to synergy. The leader becomes the focal point of the group. Unless the leader is very careful, a dependency relationship can develop between the leader and group members. An environment characterized by dependency is not conducive to synergy. Group members may defer to the leader too much. It is tempting to let the leader decide important issues. It is not uncommon for group members to compete with each other for influence over the leader.

An alternative to the person-centered approach is to view leadership as a group process. The notion behind this approach is quite simple. In order to be effective, groups need leadership, not a leader. In fact, the more leadership is shared among group members, the more effective the group is. Commitment, a function of perceived ownership, is key to the group's effectiveness. People generally like to see their own ideas work. To generate a sense of ownership in a group setting requires effective participation. The key word here is effective. Participation, to be effective, requires that the members be able to exert real influence, which may be difficult to achieve in a formal leader-follower relationship. A more fruitful approach to generating a sense of ownership is based on the awareness that certain activities must be performed if group members are to work effectively over time. These roles or activities are generally divided into two types: task and maintenance. These roles correlate with the task and maintenance issues discussed above.

Task roles
- **Initiating**: getting the group started

- **Seeking information**: drawing out information from other members

- **Giving information**: offering information to the group

- **Clarifying**: making sure the group understands what is being said

- **Summarizing**: stating what the group has done

Maintenance roles
- **Encouraging**: attempting to get members involved

- **Harmonizing**: facilitating effective conflict management

- **Setting standards**: raising the issue of proper conduct

- **Following**: acknowledging agreement or approval

- **Gatekeeping**: managing the flow of information

Each of these roles represents a potential source of influence. When group members perform one of the above roles, they are engaging in leadership. This means that leadership can be widely distributed in a group. As members feel influential, many barriers to synergy flowing from unresolved authority issues are removed. Thus, information flows more freely, resulting in a larger assembly effect.

Frequently, groups have a designated leader whether one is wanted or not. In this case, both the leader and the followers have a responsibility not to let influence issues get in the way. The leader must make a conscious effort to share leadership with other group members. The leader must not attempt to dominate the group and must actively encourage members to perform various leadership functions. The other group members must avoid always deferring to the leader and be willing to raise the leadership question as an issue that is important to the group.

Process Loss 3: We're Just One Big Happy Family

One of the most significant process losses in groups results from poorly managed conflict. Many groups develop a norm of avoiding conflict under the mistaken notion that it is always destructive. There are two problems with this approach. First, it is based on an erroneous assumption that conflict can really be avoided in a group and, secondly, it overlooks the many potential positive consequences of conflict.

The key to understanding the dynamics of conflict is the concept of interdependence. Interdependency means that there is some pattern of mutual dependency. This is certainly true of members of a group. What this means is that what other people do affects you and vice versa. A conflict process is simply inevitable in an interdependent relationship. What we experience is a series of conflict episodes in an ongoing process. As much as we would like, the process will not go away. Some episodes may be very intense while others may be very mild. Episodes may be spaced far apart, or they may occur in rapid fashion. The only thing that is sure is that they will occur. This is what makes a strategy of conflict avoidance dysfunctional.

Until recently, much was written on how to resolve conflict. The focus has now changed from resolving conflict to managing conflict. This is based largely on the acceptance of the notion that conflict cannot be resolved, particularly when interdependence is high. It is also based on the idea that conflict is not always harmful but instead has many positive outcomes. This is particularly true in relationship to synergy.

In order to manage conflict effectively, one must assume a viewpoint and a set of behaviors that differ from the way conflict is normally approached. First, one has to accept the premise that conflict is inevitable in an interdependent relationship. It is normal and need not be viewed as a sign that the group is functioning ineffectively. Secondly, one has to abandon the notion that in a conflict situation someone must lose. This is called looking at conflict as a zero-sum game, where the assumption is that the only way someone can win is at another person's expense. Such a view is very limiting and generally results in poorly managed conflict. The reason for this is the "Iron Law of Conflict" which states that in an interdependent relationship, either everybody wins or everybody loses.

Conflict that is approached from a win/lose perspective almost always ends up in a situation where everybody loses in the long run. This is because people normally do not take losing very well. Generally speaking, people may lose once or twice gracefully but then will start to put a condition on losing. The condition is that the other people also lose. This is how what started out as a win/lose outcome gets converted into a lose/lose outcome.

The Iron Law of Conflict provides a foundation for a more effective way to manage conflict. Most of us like to win when we are confronted with conflict. Losing is just no fun. The Iron Law specifies the condition for us to win and that condition is that everybody else involved in the conflict must also feel that they have won. The ways that we have traditionally approached conflict are not very helpful. Strategies such as using force, majority vote, deceit, clever negotiation, gamesmanship, and avoidance generally result in lose/lose outcomes. Even the strategy of compromise has some problems if it is used too quickly. To compromise, you have to give up something you really want. If you do not, you have not compromised. Because of this, a strategy of compromise quickly generates a lose/lose outcome. The advantage of compromise is that it avoids the many short-term negative consequences of win/lose outcomes.

The strategy that has the best chance of generating win/win outcomes is problem solving, wherein the parties involved view conflict as a mutual problem that needs to be solved. The objective of the problem solving is to find a solution that allows all parties to feel that they have won. There is room for a great deal of creativity in generating possible solutions to the problem through the use of brainstorming and other creativity techniques. A failure to do so generally results in poor solutions. For example, suppose in a group setting, Party A wants to do something one way and Party B another way. After discussing the relative merits of the two positions, a vote shows that most agree with Party A, and A's way is chosen. In addition to being a win/lose outcome, the participants have limited themselves to the merit of only those two positions. Perhaps there is a third way of doing the same thing better, that allows Party A, Party B, and other group members to feel as if they have won. But this third position is not likely to surface if the focus remains on the original two; you have to get outside the lines of the original positions.

Winning and losing are states of mind. The only person who knows what it takes for you to win is you, and the same is true for other people. Once a list of possible solutions has been generated, people should have an opportunity to say how they feel about each alternative, in hopes of finding at least one that all parties associate with winning. If not, the parties must get more creative. While this strategy may appear to be long and time consuming, it is an effective way of reducing perhaps the most significant process loss experienced by groups, namely, the hostility and energy drain associated with mismanaged conflict.

Process Loss 4: Hearing No Disagreement

Much has been written on the management of disagreement, but little has been written on the management of agreement. Did you ever find yourself going someplace with other people when, in fact, you really did not want to go? Later, you found out that nobody wanted to go, but all of you ended up there. How can this happen? From poorly managed agreement. Harvey (1974) has called the situation where a group of people end up doing something no one wants to do the "Abilene Paradox." The name comes from a personal experience of driving 53 miles in 105-degree temperature to Abilene, Texas, with a group of people, none of whom wanted to go. Harvey identified specific symptoms associated with an inability to effectively manage agreement.

- Group members agree privately, as individuals, as to the nature of the situation or problem facing the group.

- Group members agree privately, as individuals, as to the steps that would be required to cope with the situation or problem they face.

- Group members fail to communicate accurately their desires and/or beliefs to one another. In fact, they do just the opposite and thereby lead one another into misperceiving the collective reality.

- With such invalid and inaccurate information, group members make collective decisions that lead them to take actions contrary to what they want to do.

- As a result of taking actions that are counterproductive, group members experience frustration, anger, irritation, and dissatisfaction with their group.

- If the group members do not learn how to manage agreement, the cycle repeats itself with greater intensity.

The difference between this situation and one of conflict is an underlying agreement as to what should be done. The problem is that this agreement is not part of the group's reality. The key is to have each group member disclose his or her true position. While the result may be to create conflict, such disclosure is absolutely necessary to avoid the Abilene Paradox. Another strategy is to seek out group members' positions if they are not forthcoming. One of the biggest mistakes a group can make is to assume silence signifies agreement. In fact, the opposite is more likely. Silence is most likely when group members feel uncomfortable in disagreeing. A third strategy is to always check out apparent agreement. Once a group decides to do something, it must make sure that there is real agreement and not the beginning of a trip to Abilene, a great place, but not if you do not want to be there.

Interpersonal Skills and Performance

A number of suggestions have been made in this chapter about how to increase synergy and reduce process losses in a group setting. These suggestions are not easy to implement and require that group members have highly developed interpersonal skills. These include:

Active listening/clarifying
Paying attention and responding to others' ideas and feelings
Not interrupting
Asking open-ended questions
Not judging others
Summarizing and reflecting back others' ideas and feelings

Supporting/building
Accepting what others have to say
Not debating, persuading, controlling, or manipulating others
Speaking in warm, friendly terms

Creating opportunities for others to make their thoughts
and feelings known.
Building on others' ideas
Encouraging divergent points of view
Freely offering new ideas at appropriate times

Differing/confronting
Questioning one's own and others' assumptions in a
nonthreatening way
Dealing directly and specifically with apparent discrepancies
Reflecting on how the group is doing with regard to
progress, time, and personal relations

These interpersonal skills are very helpful in reducing process
losses. Groups composed of members who use these skills are more
successful in resolving the various maintenance issues and, therefore, tend to be more task-oriented sooner. They are also more effective at managing conflict and agreement. Leaders who use these
interpersonal skills are able to avoid many of the destructive
dynamics that can occur in a leader/follower relationship.

References

Harvey, J. (1974, Summer). The Abilene paradox: The management
of agreement. *Organizational Dynamics, 3* (1), 63-80.

Schutz, W. (1958). *FIRO: A three-dimensional theory of interpersonal
balance.* New York, NY: Holt, Rinehart, & Winston.

10

Spectators and Gladiators: Reconnecting the Students with the Problem

John Boehrer
Daniel J. Evans
School of Public Affairs, University of Washington

In "Bike Riding and the Art of Learning," Robert Kraft (1978) recalls that his own mastery of the two-wheeled vehicle resulted from a very focused quest for quick transportation to the candy counter at his father's store three blocks from home. The learning was halting and painful, but it was also self-directed, tenacious, and successful. Reviewing his college studies, he says that what he retained from them was not what he was told in class, but the thought he put into writing his papers, the product of his own efforts to construct meaning. Kraft goes on to relate 1) how reflecting on the connection between self, problem, and learning led him to recognize its importance to—and its usual absence from—his college students' experience, and 2) how he set about introducing it into their work A similar reorientation of one's own teaching is worth considering.

It is common to regard teaching simply as a means to convey knowledge, or perhaps skill. It seems exceptional to speak of teaching *something*. The proposition becomes more questionable when we start to talk about teaching *someone*. As teachers we face the psychological reality that we cannot actually *teach* anybody anything (Rogers, 1951). By our efforts alone, we cannot simply transfer knowledge constructed in our own experiences, or relayed by others, to our students for their genuine use. Perhaps unsettled by our inability to control the outcome of the learning process, however, we habitually act as if it were entirely the teacher's problem. We develop an Atlas complex, shouldering the entire burden of teaching and learning (Finkel & Monk, 1983). We concern ourselves with the limits of our own knowledge and focus attention on our own performance. We subordinate process to content and active engagement to coverage. We relegate students to a passive role, making them spectators when they need, and would actually prefer, to be gladiators.

But learning is not passive, something that another performs on one, like surgery. It is active; one operates on oneself. Learning is personal and purposeful: We do it to accomplish something meaningful and important to our individual selves (Cantor, 1953), anything from getting to the candy store to getting quantum mechanics. It is a natural outcome of encountering an obstacle to a goal. The desirability of achieving the goal and the possibility of overcoming the obstacle drive the learning that addresses the problem. The will to grow in ways we value continually brings us up against obstacles, and learning predictably results. In this dynamic of self-actualization, the question is not so much what stimulates learning, as we often ask in a school setting, but what constrains it.

That we cannot actually teach someone something does not, of course, mean that he or she will necessarily learn it alone. The learning may require exposure to possibilities, access to information and other resources, a structured path, guidance and encouragement, and constructive criticism. Schools and teachers can provide them. Indeed, at their most effective they provide the very problems that generate learning when linked to the students' own needs and interests. The irony of schooling, though, is that it often separates students from the experience of striving to resolve a problem for an intrinsically meaningful purpose. By focusing on solutions and answers already known, it abstracts the process of learning from the individual drive to overcome obstacles.

The structures of formal education often divert the natural flow of learning from the interaction of self and problem. The problems that prescribed curricula, and even elective courses, ask students to solve represent others' judgments of what they need to learn and lead them to acquire received wisdom instead of earned knowledge. In addition, teachers are tempted to take over the solution to the problem and ask students simply to learn the result. Gifted teachers can entertain their students by enacting the drama and passion invested in the knowledge. More ordinarily, we just present the dry results of the scholarship. Either way, we relegate the students to the galleries. It is easier to put them there, orderly and quiet, but they belong in the arena. Excluded, students accumulate solutions to problems they haven't encountered, answers to questions they haven't asked. The problem they are actually working is passing the course, getting through school (Brown et al, 1989).

Having disconnected students from the primary experience of learning by working through their own problems, we may find that a lot of teaching feels like a daunting effort to make water flow uphill, and it may escape us that everything from rivulets to torrents wants to run naturally the other way. Students who are able and willing to be engaged can bring great energy and determination to the task of learning when they get access to central, constructive process. If they are asked mainly to hear and remember, it is not surprising that either they become restless and distracted, or they perform disappointingly when papers and exams require them to do higher-order thinking. Without engagement in the problem, without some personal sense of investment in reaching a solution, the individual is poorly motivated to withstand the disturbance that accompanies genuine learning.

Students learn what they care about and remember what they understand. They may care because the material is personally relevant and interesting, because they encounter it in a challenging and intriguing way, because confronting it collaboratively with their peers is rewarding, and because working out their own construction of it is real and satisfying. Whatever the reason, their caring reestablishes the connection between self, problem, and learning. Fortunately, sharing the problem with them and engaging them in working it can start with something as simple as framing a lecture with a question and interrupting it to hear interim answers. More productively, it can go on to supplant some lectures with group tasks. More elaborately, it can extend to running case discussions or full-scale simulations.

Bringing students into the arena need not imply a total revision of one's teaching, but it does involve a shift of emphasis from the exposition of knowledge to the recasting of what we know into questions to be resolved, issues to be grappled with, problems to be worked, mysteries to be unraveled. The shift involves recognizing the contrast between knowledge, a commodity that we can imagine being transferred or conveyed, and knowing, a living experience that we understand can belong only to the person having it. More important than the teacher's delivering the product of his or her own learning is the function of creating and maintaining an environment in which students will learn to work (O'Hare, 1989).

Effective as this approach is, both students and faculty may resist it. They need to confront and conquer the collusion to avoid the effort and the risk that it entails. There is a bad bargain that teachers and students can and often do make, and it is to the effect of, "I won't ask much of you if you don't ask much of me." This agreement to accept less learning for less work on both sides has several sources. To engage students more thoroughly requires teachers to become more personally involved, which produces a vulnerability they (the teachers) may find uncomfortable (Weimer, 1990). On the students' side, genuine learning implies exchange and requires students to withstand confusion and disturbance (Cantor, 1953). The students may resist the unfamiliar demand for greater involvement and higher-order thinking when it counters the expectation that previous schooling has led them to develop.

Yet experience wears away resistance. The rewards of playing a more central and responsible role in working the problem are substantial and apparent in both the process and the outcome of learning (Jackson & Prosser, 1989). Active engagement in personally involving work that leads to genuine understanding creates its own demand, one that a teacher may sometimes find challenging to meet. Coming out of the spectator's seat may require overcoming some inertia, but being the gladiator, with all the exertion and risk it entails, compares with spectating as a three-dimensional reality with a two-dimensional representation. Learning is, after all, the students' problem, not because their progress and welfare do not concern us, but simply because they alone can actually solve it. The more centrally we can engage them in the learning process, the more personally we can involve them in it, the more teaching we will be able to do. Recognizing that it is not our mastery of the material, but the students' struggle with it that is the issue, we can remember to keep their experiences at the center of the process, not our own (Cantor, 1953). We can also remind ourselves that we are not simply trying to get them through school, or supply them with important knowledge, but to teach them to work the overarching problem, which is learning itself, for themselves. The farther they go, the more important it becomes to involve them in monitoring and directing their own learning. In the end, we are concerned not only about the knowledge they carry away, but even more about the capacity they take with them for learning on their own throughout life.

References

Brown, J. S., Collins, A., & Duguid, P. (1989). Situated cognition and the culture of learning. *Educational Researcher, 18* (1), 32-42.

Cantor, N. (1953). *The teaching-learning process.* New York, NY: Holt, Rinehart, & Winston.

Finkel, D. L., & Monk, G. S. (1983). Teachers and learning groups: Dissolution of the Atlas Complex. In C. Bouton & R. Y. Garth (Eds.), *Learning in groups.* San Francisco, CA: Jossey-Bass.

Jackson, M. W., & Prosser, M. T. (1989). Less lecturing, more lecturing. *Studies in Higher Education, 14* (1).

Kraft, R. G. (1978). Bike riding and the art of learning. *Change, 10* (6).

O'Hare, M. (1989). *Teaching and formal models.* Unpublished paper.

Rogers, C. R. (1951). *Client-centered therapy.* Boston, MA: Houghton-Mifflin.

Weimer, M. (1990). *Improving college teaching: Strategies for developing instructional effectiveness.* San Francisco, CA: Jossey-Bass.

This article originally appeared in a 1990–1991 issue of Teaching Excellence: Toward the Best in the Academy, *a publication of The Professional and Organizational Development Network in Higher Education. Reprinted with permission.*

11

Betty Miles's Worst Nightmare: A Cooperative Learning Dilemma

Barbara J. Millis
Director of Faculty Development, US Air Force Academy

A Case Study

"Hi, I'm Betty Miles," smiled the tall, dark-haired instructor near the door. "Welcome to Modern Children's Literature."

Students clutching *Charlotte's Web* and other weighty tomes, some glancing nervously at their watches, scurried into the classroom, eyeing the orderly desks arrayed with thick packets of materials. As the greetings continued, they arranged their book bags, purses, and notebooks, and most of them began thumbing through the 13-page syllabus. After a few minutes, they noticed the course information neatly printed on the board with the instructor's name and the instructions asking them to complete a personal data sheet included with the syllabus material.

At 1:05 p.m. when 24 students were in place, Betty Miles walked to the front of the room and called the class to order.

"Are the brothers Grimm too grim for children?" she asked rhetorically. "Do you want your preteen reading *Dinky Hocker Shoots Smack?* This semester we'll be exploring these and other issues in the far-from-childish world of children's literature. Before we begin our discussions, however, I'd like us to get better acquainted. If you haven't already done so, could you please complete the pink Personal Data Sheet on top of your syllabus while I put the afternoon's agenda on the board. Also, please be prepared to move to a different seat in five minutes."

Several students looked puzzled, but most dutifully scribbled on their pink sheets. Of the 24 students, all but six were women, ranging in age from fresh-faced teenagers to a grandmotherly-type sitting in the back row. One of the males, a short, soft-featured man in his early 30s, sported a single gold earring.

"As you can see by the agenda," said Betty, "we will now begin with an icebreaker called the three-step interview. After that, we'll cover the course objectives and requirements, and then we'll begin our exploration of trends and issues in children's literature. We'll conclude promptly at 1:50 p.m. Are there any questions about what we'll do today?"

After waiting expectantly but finding no hands raised, Betty explained the interview process. "I want each of you to identify someone in the room who seems unlike you, someone perhaps of a different gender, age, or race. The person with the shortest hair will begin by asking interview questions of the other partner. I've put four suggested questions on the board. The most important are 'Why are you taking this course? What do you hope to get out of it?' Interview for two minutes. Then, when I ring this little bell," she demonstrated it, "switch roles and have the other person ask the same questions. Then, when you hear the bell again, each pair should find another pair, making a foursome. For the next five minutes, introduce your partners to the group so that you all know each other by the end of the session. Don't try to repeat all you have learned during the pair introduction. Just concentrate on the most interesting points. Are the instructions clear?" Betty looked around. "Okay, begin."

The room filled with milling people suddenly engaged in animated conversations. Betty moved skillfully around the room, making certain that each person had a partner. About halfway through the exercise three students straggled in, but she carefully paired two of them and integrated the third into a circle of four just forming.

As the time expired, Betty rang the bell, but the room was still filled with noise and laughter.

Betty, anticipating this response, now flicked the lights and, finally, brought the class to attention.

"We need a quiet signal," she announced, "to bring order from anarchy because we'll be working in groups a lot this semester. It could be anything that will bring you to attention, but we need to create a ripple effect. For example, if you choose a raised hand, whenever one of you sees a hand raised, you need to finish your sentence and raise your hand. The room can come to order that way in less than 30 seconds."

"A raised hand seems too childish," said a tall, blond girl in a checked sundress. "How about flashing the 'V for victory' sign?"

"That's a good idea," chimed another.

"Okay, if we're in agreement," said Betty. "We'll make that our signal. Often, I'll use both the victory sign and the bell. Please stay with your new team, and let's begin our discussion of the syllabus." Betty carefully explained all aspects of the course, including the journal assignments, the reading cards due every third class period, the chapter reading quizzes, and the book shares. Students asked few questions, but one studious-looking girl with glasses said, "Wow, this is a lot more work than I expected."

During the discussion, Betty emphasized the importance of teamwork and cooperation. "You will help each other learn," she emphasized. "Next week I'll put you in assigned learning teams where you can coach one another over the chapter material, but each of you will take the quizzes individually. Each of you on a high-achieving team will get a bonus point for each five points the team, as a whole, improves over the last quiz."

Betty glanced at her watch. "This team approach may be new to you. There's time, I think, for me to get your reactions. Let's do an exercise called 'Numbered Heads.' Could you please call out numbers one, two, three, four—in your current teams—so that everyone has a number. Go ahead—anyone can start. " Class members glanced uncertainly at one another, but soon cries of "one, two, three, four" reverberated throughout the room.

Betty smiled approvingly. "Good work! I'd like you to take the next seven minutes to talk as a team about your feelings about the course. When you see the quiet signal or hear the bell, I'll ask about three of you to share your responses with the entire group. I will call on you by number to represent not your own opinion, but the team's consensus. You won't know which number I will call, so I hope that all of you will pay attention, summarizing the discussion so that you can present an accurate assessment of the team thinking. Those of you who rarely speak out in classes should feel more comfortable at giving a team response. Okay, begin."

The buzz sessions went smoothly. Betty moved rapidly among the groups, trying to remain as unobtrusive as possible. One group, in fact, was involved in such a heated discussion that they did not notice her poised confidently at a desk outside the perimeter of their circle. As she listened to their remarks, however, Betty's confidence began to evaporate.

The man with the earring had obviously been speaking for several minutes: "I think it sucks," he said. "I'm here to get a good grade. Period. I don't want to have to wade through all this 'hold-me touch-me feel-me' crap. I'm sorry to sound so negative, but I paid good tuition money to get three credits of upper-level English out of the way. This looked like an easy course, and I was willing to tolerate a little 'Mary Has a Little Lamb' garbage during lectures, but now I feel like I'm expected to spill my guts on the Phil Donahue show."

A plump, brown-eyed young woman spoke next: "Well, I don't mind cooperating. In fact, I think it's a good idea. In too many of my classes I've felt like a Social Security number. The grade is the problem for me. I heard the teacher say that the cooperative learning grade works like bonus points. It can't hurt us. But frankly, I'm skeptical. What if half you guys—you, for example, John—don't show up or you don't do the work. I'm stuck with freeloaders no matter how hard I work."

"Yeah, that bugs me, too, " said another young woman. "In my last class the teacher dumped us in teams, and I did all the work. I wrote the whole group project on my own. The other students seemed to sense that I would do it. I don't know why I did it—the grade I guess—but I also liked our topic on homeless people. I didn't get any help from the teacher, either, and that bothered me even more. He seemed preoccupied with some survey he was conducting on the urban poor."

"The same stuff happened to me," said the woman in the sundress "Group work, no matter what fancy name you give it, seems a cop out. The teacher doesn't have to do any work. She expects us to share resources and ideas. What if we can only pool our own ignorance? I'm really—uh—nervous about this class."

Betty slipped away to the next team, but her mind stayed focused on the conversation she had just overheard. What should she do? She immediately considered the question of whether or not she should call on someone from the last team to share their responses. But she wondered, also, if other people in the class were feeling so negative. How could she turn this situation around?

Focus Questions

1. What was your first impression of Betty's class?

2. Were the students justified in their opposition to group work?

3. Should Betty call on someone from the disgruntled group?

4. What can Betty do during this class session to turn this situation around?

5. What should she do during the next class period?

6. What arguments in favor of structured small-group work (cooperative learning) might convince dualistic thinkers to "buy into" it?

7. The next time Betty offers this course, what should she do differently?

This case study originally appeared in Millis, B. J. (1994). Conducting cooperative cases. In E. C. Wadsworth (Ed.), To improve the academy: Resources for faculty, instructional, & organizational development *(Vol.13) (pp. 309-320). Stillwater, OK: New Forums Press. Reprinted with permission.*

Selected
Annotated References

Cottell, P. G., Jr., & Millis, B. J. (1994). Complex cooperative learning structures for college and university courses. In E. C. Wadsworth (Ed.), *To improve the academy: Resources for student, faculty, and organizational development* (vol. 13) (pp. 285–308). Stillwater, OK: New Forums Press.

This practical article describes a number of techniques for use with small groups. The techniques include structured learning teams, ways of using a deck of playing cards to facilitate team structure and organization, the jigsaw, structured controversy, guided reciprocal peer questioning, and structures for student critiquing.

Davis, B. G. (1993). *Tools for teaching.* San Francisco, CA: Jossey-Bass.

Chapter 18 in this useful book is "Collaborative Learning: Group Work and Study Teams." In addition to a general but helpful introduction, the chapter includes sections on general strategies, designing group work, organizing learning groups, guiding learning groups, evaluating group work, dealing with student and faculty concerns about group work, and setting up study teams.

Fiechtner, S. B., & Davis, E. A. (1984-85). Why some groups fail: A survey of students' experiences with learning groups. *The Organizational Behavior Teaching Review, 2* (4), 58–71.

This article is based on a survey distributed in several upper-division speech communication and business policy courses at two major southwestern universities. The analysis gives recommendations on group structure, group size, type and number of group activities, in-class and out-of-class group work, and the grading system. It also discusses how to avoid problems and presents a table of what *not* to do in groups.

Goodsell, A. S., et al. (1992). *Collaborative learning: A sourcebook for higher education*. University Park, PA: National Center on Post-secondary Teaching, Learning, and Assessment.

The four sections of this helpful sourcebook include articles that define and describe collaborative learning, explain how collaborative learning is implemented, discuss the research on collaborative learning, and describe where collaborative learning is used. Each section contains an annotated bibliography as well as a general bibliography. The section on implementation includes a discipline-specific bibliography.

Gould, P., & Gould, R. (Writers). (1988). *From "No" to "Yes"—The constructive route to agreement* [videotape]. (Available from Dumbarton House, 68 Oxford St. London, W1N 9LA. Phone: 1-800-861-4246. web site: http://www.videoarts.com/ or http://www.coastal.com/)

Martin, a tense and stubborn manager, learns to listen actively and improve his negotiating techniques. This video goes beyond basic listening skills and effectively illustrates group conflict resolution. It demonstrates active listening, explaining one's feelings, and working to a joint solution. (27 minutes)

Johnson, D. W., Johnson, R. T., & Smith, K. A. (1991). *Cooperative learning: Increasing college faculty instructional productivity.* Washington, DC: The George Washington University's School of Education and Human Development. (ASHE-ERIC Higher Education Report No. 4)

In this book, the authors pull together most of their previous writing on cooperative learning at the college level. Chapters include information on the basic aspects of cooperative learning, research on cooperative learning, the role of the instructor, information on using various strategies, and cooperation among faculty. The book also includes a chapter on base groups.

Johnson, D. W., Johnson, R. T., & Smith, K. A. (1998, July/August). Cooperative learning returns to college: What evidence is there that it works? *Change, 30* (4), 26–35.

The authors define cooperative learning and discuss the theories behind it. They also explain the dynamics that make it work and present a summary of the research. Lastly, the article describes ways of using cooperative learning in college classes.

Kagan, S. (1992). *Cooperative learning.* San Juan Capistrano, CA: Kagan Cooperative Learning.

This book is a comprehensive handbook on cooperative learning for teachers. It covers cooperative learning theory and learning methods, structures, lesson designs, conflict resolution, and classroom management.

Matthews, R. S., Cooper, J. L., et al. (1995, July/August). Building bridges between cooperative and collaborative learning. *Change, 27* (4), 35–40.

The authors compare collaborative and cooperative learning as practiced in higher education classes. The article also includes an annotated list of materials for additional reading on collaborative and cooperative learning.

Meyers, C., & Jones, T. B. (1993). *Promoting active learning: Strategies for the college classroom.* San Francisco, CA: Jossey-Bass.

Two chapters in this book deal with teams in the classroom: Chapter Four, titled "Informal Small Groups," has sections on what happens in small groups, the purpose of small groups, structuring groups for success, and managing the classroom for small groups. The chapter also has a "teaching tip" section on disagreeing without put-downs and a sample teaching model for using small groups in a large lecture class. Chapter Five, "Cooperative Student Projects" includes material on the key elements that Johnson and Johnson stress when using cooperative groups. The chapter also has a section on the purposes of cooperative student projects and presents some teaching models in the section "Structuring Cooperative Projects for Success."

Michaelson, L. K. (1992). Team learning: A comprehensive approach for harnessing the power of small groups in higher education. In D. H. Wulff & J. D. Nyquist (Eds.),*To improve the academy: Resources for student, faculty, and organizational development* (Vol.11) (pp. 107–122). Stillwater, OK: New Forums Press.

Michaelson describes a group-based approach to team learning that has a specific instructional activity sequence. The approach was originally used to facilitate active learning in large classes, but the author has found it effective in a wide variety of educational settings.

Millis, B. J. (1990). Helping faculty build learning communities through cooperative groups. In L. Hilsen (Ed.),*To improve the academy: Resources for student, faculty, and organizational development* (Vol. 9) (pp. 43–58). Stillwater, OK: New Forums Press.

Millis defines cooperative learning, presents some cooperative learning strategies, includes a discussion of the research on cooperative learning, and discusses its value by noting that it helps to create a sense of community when teaching a student population that is diverse in numerous ways.

Nilson, L. B. (1998*) Teaching at its best: A research-based resource for college instructors*. Bolton, MA: Anker.

In one informative chapter, Nilson reviews the research on cooperative learning, discusses the role shifts required for cooperative learning, analyzes the crucial elements of cooperative learning, gives management tips, and provides a sampler of cooperative learning strategies.

Riordan, D., Street, D. L., & Roof, B. M. (1997). *Group learning: Applications in higher education.* Harrisonburg, VA: Institute for Research in Higher Education.

This volume contains a number of articles that represent current higher education literature on using group learning techniques. The first section has introductory articles on group learning techniques, including "Research on Cooperative Learning: Consensus and Controversy" by Robert E. Slavin. The second section contains four applications of cooperative learning in the college classroom; the third section addresses issues of designing groups such as self-selection and gender mix. The final section includes research articles on group performance and retention.

Slavin, R. (1995). *Cooperative learning: Theory, research, and practice.* Boston, MA: Allyn and Bacon.

Slavin discusses cooperative learning theory and research, includes handy guides for cooperative learning methods, and provides information on other cooperative learning methods and resources. The book, according to Slavin, is primarily intended for preservice and inservice courses and workshops with teachers or future teachers.

Tiberius, R. G. (1995). *Small group teaching: A trouble-shooting guide* (Monograph Series No. 22). The Ontario Institute for Studies in Education.

This book focuses on teaching a class that is a small group as opposed to dividing a class into teams for various projects, but it also contains ideas for teams, for example, the use of buzz groups, learning cells, POPS, brainstorming groups, and debate. The guide is divided into three main parts: group goals, group interaction, and group motivation and emotion. Each topic includes chapters that describe a problem, give possible causes for the problem, and suggestions to remedy the problem.

Web site: http://bestpractice.net/

Many faculty development centers include resources for cooperative or team learning on their sites. This site is devoted to cooperative learning and is funded jointly by Arizona State University, Cal Poly Pomona, and the Fund for Improvement in Postsecondary Education (FIPSE). The site includes teaching materials, bibliographies, resources and links, and a listserv.

References

Astin, A. (1993). *What matters in college: Four critical years revisited.* San Francisco, CA: Jossey-Bass.

Bandura, A. J. (1971). *Social learning theory.* New York, NY: General Learning Press.

Bazerman, C. (1988). *Shaping written knowledge: The genre and activity of the experimental article in science.* Madison, WI: University of Wisconsin Press.

Bazerman, C. (Ed.). (1991). *Textual dynamics of the professions: Historical and contemporary studies of writing in professional communities.* Madison, WI: University of Wisconsin Press.

Brown, J. S., Collins, A., & Duguid, P. (1989). Situated cognition and the culture of learning. *Educational Researcher, 18* (1), 32-42.

Bruffee, K. A. (1999). *Collaborative learning: Higher education, interdependence, and the authority of knowledge.* Baltimore, MD: Johns Hopkins University Press.

Byrnes, D. A., & Kiger, G. (Eds.). (1996). *Common bonds: Anti-bias teaching in a diverse society* (2nd ed.). Wheaton, MD: Association for Childhood Education International.

Cantor, N. (1953). *The teaching-learning process.* New York, NY: Holt, Rinehart, & Winston.

Clawson, M., & Clouse, L. (1998, November). Service learning as a teaching strategy in human development and family studies courses. *Family Science Review, 11* (4), 336–353.

Cooper, J., et al. (1990). *Cooperative learning and college instruction: Effective use of student learning teams.* Long Beach, CA: University Academic Publications Program.

Cooper, J. L., Robinson, P., & McKinney, M. (1994). Cooperative learning in the classroom. In D. F. Halpern (Ed.), *Changing college classrooms* (pp. 77-79). San Francisco, CA: Jossey-Bass.

Cuseo, J. B. (1991). *The freshman orientation seminar: A research-based rationale for its value, delivery, and content.* (The Freshman Year Experience Monograph Series No. 4). University of South Carolina, National Resource Center for the Freshman Year Experience.

Davis, B. G. (1993). *Tools for teaching.* San Francisco, CA: Jossey-Bass.

Finkel, D. L., & Monk, G. S. (1983). Teachers and learning groups: Dissolution of the Atlas Complex. In C. Bouton & R. Y. Garth (Eds.), *Learning in groups.* San Francisco, CA: Jossey-Bass.

Fosnot, C. T. (Ed.). (1996). *Constructivism: Theory, perspectives, and practice.* New York, NY: Teachers College Press.

Frierson, H. T. (1986). Two intervention methods: Effects on groups of predominantly black nursing students' board scores. *Journal of Research and Development in Education, 19*, 18–23.

Gabelnick, F., MacGregor, J., Matthews, R. S., & Smith, B. L. (1992). Learning communities and general education. *Perspectives, 22* (1), 104-121.

Graves, N., & Graves, T. (1989). Should we teach cooperative skills as a part of each cooperative lesson? *Cooperative Learning, 10* (2), 19–20.

Green, L. W., & Krueter, M. W. (1999). *Health promotion planning: An educational and ecological approach* (3rd ed.). Mountain View, CA: Mayfield.

Hacker, D. (1997). *A pocket style manual* (2nd ed.). Boston, MA: Bedford Books.

Hacker, D. (1999). *A writer's reference* (4th ed.). Boston, MA: Bedford/St. Martins.

Harvey, J. (1974, Summer). The Abilene paradox: The management of agreement. *Organizational Dynamics, 3* (1), 63-80.

Hill, P. J. (1985). *The rationale for learning communities.* Paper presented at the Inaugural Conference of the Washington Center for Improving the Quality of Undergraduate Education, Olympia, WA.

Jackson, M. W., & Prosser, M. T. (1989). Less lecturing, more lecturing. *Studies in Higher Education, 14* (1).

Johnson, D. W., Johnson, R. T., & Smith, K. A. (1991). *Cooperative learning: Increasing college faculty instructional productivity.* Washington, DC: The George Washington University, School of Education and Human Development. (ASHE-ERIC Higher Education Report No. 4)

Johnson, D. W., Johnson, R. T., & Smith, K. A. (1998). *Active learning: Co-Operation in the college classroom* (2nd ed.). Edina, MN: Interaction Book Co.

Kirby, M. (Ed.). (1965). *Happenings: An illustrated anthology.* New York, NY: E. P. Dutton.

Kraft, R. G. (1978). Bike riding and the art of learning. *Change, 10* (6).

Lawrence, G. A. (1988). *The zig-zag process for problem solving.* Gainesville, FL: Center for the Application of Psychological Type.

McGraw-Hill Primis. (1992). White-collar and business crime: Regulation of business through the criminal process. In Whitman & Gergacz, *The legal environment of business* (pp. 164-165). New York, NY: McGraw-Hill.

McKenna, S. (1995). The business impact of management attitudes toward dealing with conflict: A cross-cultural assessment. *Journal of Managerial Psychology, 10* (7).

Meyers, C., & Jones, T. B. (1993). *Promoting active learning strategies for the college classroom.* San Francisco, CA: Jossey-Bass.

Millis, B. J. (1994). Conducting cooperative cases. In E. C. Wadsworth (Ed.), *To improve the academy: Resources for faculty, instructional, & organizational development* (Vol.13) (pp. 309-320). Stillwater, OK: New Forums Press.

Millis, B. (1994, Spring). Increasing thinking through cooperative writing. *Cooperative Learning and College Teaching, 4* (3), 7-8.

O'Hare, M. (1989). *Teaching and formal models.* Unpublished.

Pasadena Art Museum. (1967). *Allan Kaprow.* An exhibition sponsored by the Art Alliance of the Pasadena Art Museum, Pasadena, CA.

Rogers, C. R. (1951). *Client-centered therapy.* Boston, MA: Houghton-Mifflin.

Rosa, A., & Eschholz, P. (1996). *The writer's brief handbook* (2nd ed.). Boston, MA: Allyn & Bacon.

Rosser, S. (1998, Summer). Group work in science, engineering, and mathematics: Consequences of ignoring gender and race. *College Teaching, 64* (3), 82–88.

Schön, D. A. (1983). *The reflective practitioner: How professionals think in action.* New York, NY: Basic Books.

Schön, D. A. (1987). *Educating the reflective practitioner: Toward a new design for teaching and learning in the professions.* San Francisco, CA: Jossey-Bass.

Schutz, W. (1958). *FIRO: A three dimensional theory of interpersonal balance.* New York, NY: Holt, Rinehart, & Winston.

Sharan, S., & Sharan, Y. (1992). *Expanding cooperative learning through group investigation.* New York, NY: Teachers College Press.

Smith, B. L. (1991). Taking structure seriously: The learning community model. *Liberal Education, 77* (2), 42–48.

Thomas, K. W., & Kilmann, R. H. (1974). *The Thomas-Kilmann confict mode instrument.* Tuxedo, NY: Xicom.

Tinto, V., & Riemer, S. (1998). *Learning communities and the reconstruction of remedial education in higher education.* From material prepared for a presentation at the Conference on Replacing Remediation in Higher Education at Stanford University, January 26–27, 1998, sponsored by the Ford Foundation and the United States Department of Education.

Treisman, P. U. (1983). Improving the performance of minority students in college-level mathematics. *Innovation Abstracts, 5* (17).

Tuckman, B. (1965). Developmental sequence in small groups. *Psychological Bulletin, 63* (6), 384–399.

Tuckman, B., & Jensen, M. A. C. (1977). Stages of small-group development revisited. *Group and Organizational Studies, 2* (4), 419–427.

Watkins, B. T. (1989, June 14). Many campuses now challenging minority students to excel in math and science. *Chronicle of Higher Education, 35* (40), A13,16–17. (ERIC NO: EJ390853)

Weimer, M. (1990). *Improving college teaching: Strategies for developing instructional effectiveness.* San Francisco, CA: Jossey-Bass.

White, J. B. (1985). *Heracles' bow: Essays on the rhetoric and poetics of the law.* Madison, WI: University of Wisconsin Press.

Index